On the Trail of Sea Turtles

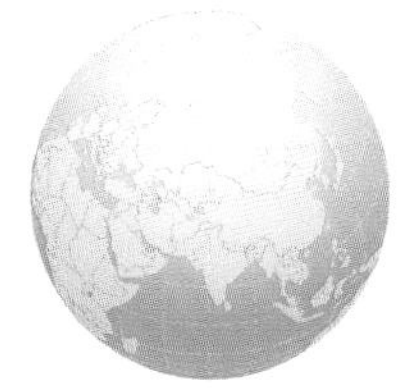

On the Trail of Sea Turtles

Bernard DEVAUX and Bernard DE WETTER

Illustrations by Maël DEWYNTER

Contents

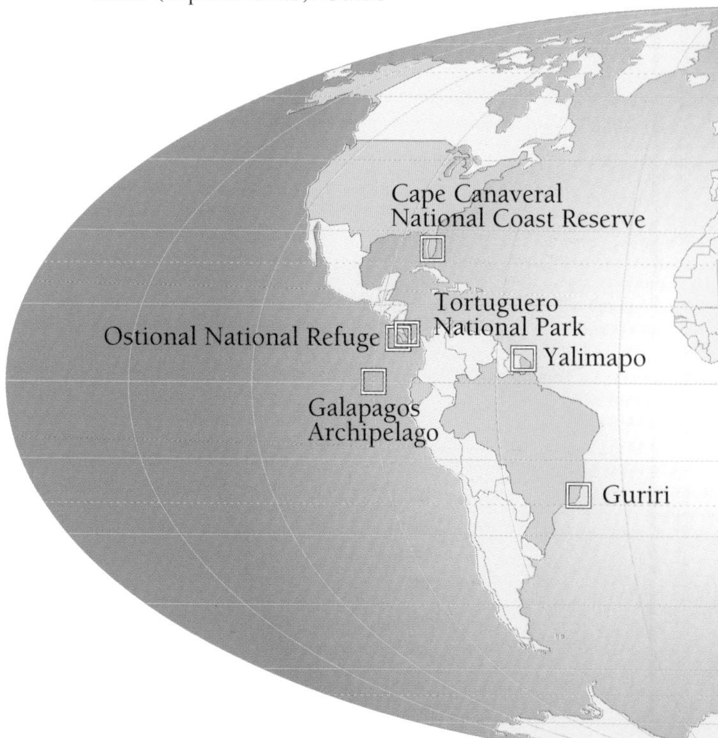

Cape Canaveral
National Coast Reserve
Tortuguero
National Park
Ostional National Refuge
Yalimapo
Galapagos
Archipelago
Guriri

Ra's al Hadd
Bhitar Kanika Sanctuary
Rantau Abang
Bentota Beach
Grand Comoro and Mayotte
Bundaberg Beach

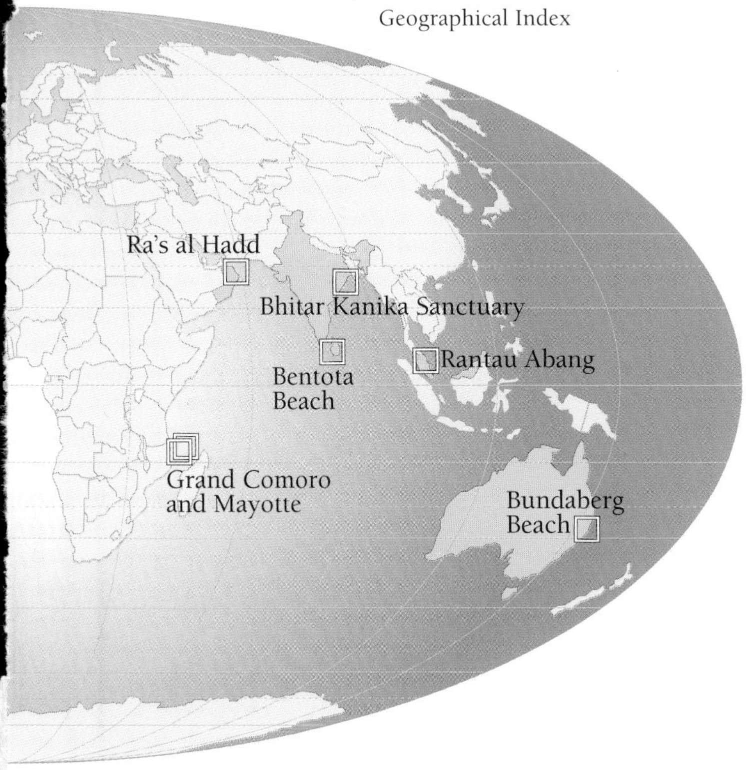

Foreword

For thousands of years, sea turtles have arrived on the beaches of tropical and subtropical regions of the world to complete the most important act for the survival of their species.

Observing sea turtles laying their eggs is a fascinating experience; being present when these animals from another age appear, leaving the secret world of the sea to once again make contact with land for a few hours during the night, leaves an unforgettable impression. This is the unique spectacle that we are inviting you to witness.

Sea turtles are great travelers; evolving in the vast world of the ocean, they spread their nesting sites throughout most of the "hot" regions of the two hemispheres. The beaches that each year welcome the nocturnal ballet of these remarkable reptiles number in the thousands.

From among all the sites that exist we have therefore tried to choose some on each continent, in order to present as broad a range as possible. We have also preferred those sites where the observation of egg laying is structured, regulated, or organized. This choice of sites guarantees you the optimum number of opportunities for viewing under good conditions this fabulous phenomenon of egg laying. In some cases, you will also benefit from the presence of avid specialists who may teach you a great deal about the habits of sea turtles, their status, and the dangers that threaten their future. Armed with this information, the interested reader may then explore independently other areas known for egg laying; it will be possible to take advantage of this extraordinary spectacle with full knowledge of the facts, without disturbing these particularly shy animals. The security aspect must also be mentioned—in places where poachers are active, sometimes in very organized, very efficient gangs, it may be dangerous to venture unaccompanied.

Finally, we have attached only secondary importance to the possibilities of observing sea turtles in the element in which they spend almost their entire existence—the sea—as this type of observation is reserved almost exclusively for divers. The latter may find them in all tropical seas throughout the world, particularly in shallow areas rich in marine vegetation, as well as in coral reefs, where sea turtles find abundant food supplies.

Note

The world changes and evolves quickly. The information that we are giving you here is based on the most reliable data available at the time this text is being edited. However, conditions that prevail in the areas presented here may have changed considerably by the time you read this, particularly as a result of the inherently unstable nature of the coastline in certain areas—beach erosion, the appearance of sandbanks, and so on. The installation of certain tourist facilities may also compromise the possibilities for observation. This is the case with the beaches in the Lara area of Cyprus, which are currently being threatened, in spite of their status as protected zones, by the construction of a vast hotel complex, and may disappear as reproduction sites in the very near future if the protests and actions taken by ecologists should fail. On the other hand, the progressive improvement of protection measures, and the means for visiting in several protected areas on the coasts of Florida in recent years have made it possible to considerably increase the possibilities of seeing turtles (loggerhead and green sea turtles). Also, the Sultanate of Oman, sealed to foreign visitors as of several years ago, now offers rather exceptional possibilities for the observation of sea turtles.

We cannot, therefore, formally and absolutely guarantee the observations as we are describing them in this work.

INTRODUCTION TO SEA TURTLES

In Sipahan, Malaysia, sea turtles are the dominant species. A true underwater sanctuary brings together hundreds of chelonians.

Origin and Evolution

The first vertebrates, the tetrapods, appeared approximately 400 million years ago. These are what we today call the batrachians, faithful to the marine environment. About 60 million years later, the cotylosaurians appeared; they may be considered the ancestors of all reptiles. It was perhaps the cotylosaurians that first laid an egg in a shell on land, thus freeing themselves from the marine world.

At the beginning of the Triassic period, 260 million years ago, there appeared the *Captorhinus*, a small lizard approximately 2 feet (60 cm) long, the first vertebrate with scapulae inside the rib cage. This feature made it possible for the sides of these animals to develop in a bony casing. The reptiles that followed were covered with bony nodules, which still existed in the *Proganichelys*, 230 million years ago, believed to be the ancestor of all turtles. Its body is covered with a bony carapace. At that point, two groups separated in the Jurassic period (195 million years ago) to form the

Skeleton of an *Archelon*, a fossil sea turtle, 16 feet (5 m) long and weighing 3 metric tons.

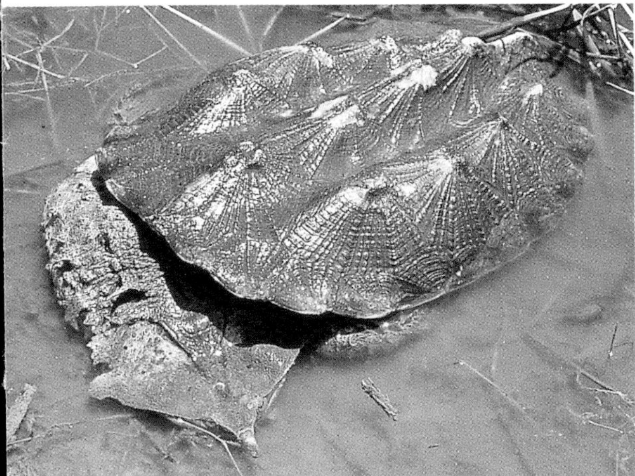

Some turtles, such as the mata-mata of South America, have necks that bend horizontally (pleurodires), unlike sea turtles, whose necks bend vertically (cryptodires).

pleurodires, whose neck folds back horizontally, and the cryptodires, whose neck folds back vertically. Sea turtles are part of the latter group.

Originally, turtles were terrestrial; then, 100 million years later, some adapted to the aquatic environment, and 50 million years later, to the marine environment. It can thus be said that modern-day sea turtles descended from lines that have existed for more than 80 million years. Originally, there were five families of sea turtles; today there are only two.

General Description

Turtles have hardly changed since *Proganochelys*. Their **carapace** corresponds with the development of the sides of the animal; it consists of a back, a front, and two bridges that join them laterally, forming excellent protection against

The *cistudes* of Europe *(Emys orbicularis)* represent the most recently evolved line in the order of chelonians. This is a small turtle—7.1 inches (18 cm)—found in the south of France.

predators and variations in temperature. But the 260 species of turtles that exist today have changed, and this carapace is sometimes transformed into a thin and flexible skin, as in the "soft turtles," or a coat of leather, as in the leatherback sea turtle, which thus has greater mobility than its fellow creatures. This skin has an underlayer of somewhat developed bony nodules that are the vestiges of the original carapace.

The **weight** of the chelonians is variable, ranging for adult animals from 2.8 pounds (80 g) in a small South African species *(Homopus signatus)* to 2,090 pounds (950 kg) for the leatherback sea turtle, one of the most remarkable turtles on earth. The lightest of the sea turtles, Kemp's Ridley sea turtle, weighs 99 pounds (45 kg).

The **organs** of the chelonians are like those of the majority of vertebrates. Their neck consists of eight vertebrae and can fold back, more or less, inside the carapace. The necks of sea turtles have little mobility, and are almost rigid in the leatherback sea turtle, because high speed movement in water requires a certain resistance. Chelonians do not have teeth, which have been replaced by a cutting beak. They do not have external ears but, the internal ear under the auditory plate is efficient. Finally, turtles have only one orifice for excretion, which is also used for reproduction. The male penis extends from here; in females, the orifice serves as an intromission canal. Females have two oviducts, and it has been noted that sperm may live there, in a latent state, for several years.

The lungs of these animals, identical to our own, require the sea turtle to breathe every ten minutes—or less according to the activity—and the animal must return frequently to the surface. They can be heard breathing noisily on the surface of the sea; at this moment, they can be caught by fishermen. At rest, their lungs are full of air, while man exhales; the lungs serve the turtles as a ballast, and an oxygen reserve for diving. As sea turtles do not have mobile sides, they cannot use their rib cage for breathing. The muscles of their fore flippers and their internal organs activate the lungs.

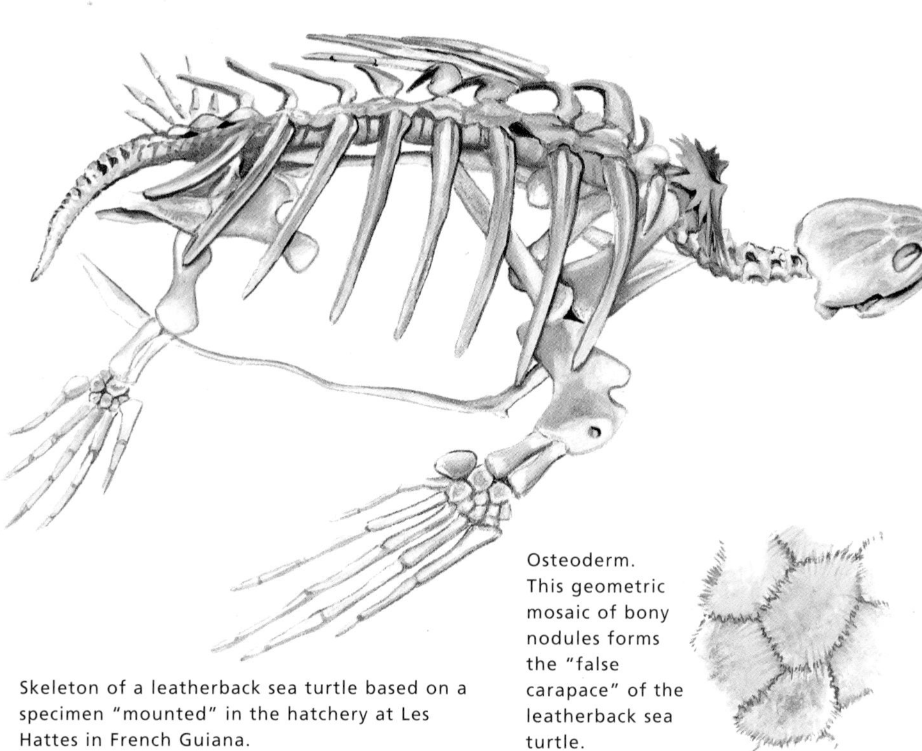

Skeleton of a leatherback sea turtle based on a specimen "mounted" in the hatchery at Les Hattes in French Guiana.

Osteoderm. This geometric mosaic of bony nodules forms the "false carapace" of the leatherback sea turtle.

The **senses** of sea turtles are similar to our own. The sense of smell seems to be weak, but eyesight is good, especially in water turtles that seem to have better distance vision than land turtles. Hearing seems particularly acute in sea turtles, except perhaps in the leatherback sea turtle; even asleep on the surface, they can clearly hear the slightest noise made by the oar of an approaching fisherman. They possess both a middle and an inner ear, but to date little is known about the limits of their audible range. The directional sense is also well developed in some turtles, and sea turtles demonstrate a remarkable talent for navigating long distances. Their capacity to orient themselves over very long distances may be due to the magnetite particles present in their cells, but they also seem to make use of the position of the stars, the moon, and the sun, the direction of marine currents, and even the saltiness of the water. Their ability to once again find a natal beach at the opposite end of the world has always been amazing to humans. Leatherback sea turtles that regularly lay their eggs in Les Hattes, French Guiana, are also regularly seen in West Africa; others migrate from the Galapagos to Malaysia. The sea turtle, obviously, is a marvelous aquatic machine at ease in all the warm waters of the globe.

The mating of giant land turtles, such as these two *Geochelone sulcata,* is always noisy and spectacular. The male weighs 220 pounds (100 kg), while the female weighs no more than 132 pounds (60 kg).

Sexual dimorphism, pronounced in land turtles, is less visible in sea turtles. The male is sometimes smaller than the female, and has a very long and wide tail, which makes it possible to recognize him when the animals swim in a group. In loggerhead turtles, for instance, the tail of the female does not extend beyond the rear edge of the carapace, while that of the male does. In some species, males have a rather powerful claw at the joint of the front flipper, with which they can attach themselves on the back of females. The position of the cloaca varies according to sex: closer to the abdomen in females, further toward the end of the tail in males. This enables the male to position his hemipenis for insertion during mating. Finally, male sea turtles are never seen on land, since only females return to land in order to lay eggs. The males are seen offshore, waiting for the females to return to the sea to mate with them.

It is very rare to witness sea turtles (seen here, two green sea turtles) mating outside the water. Generally, the males wait for the females opposite the nesting sites and fertilize them when they return to the sea.

Metabolism

Reptiles differ from mammals and birds in the fact that they are ectotherms; that is to say, they depend up to a point on the external temperature for the thermal balance of their metabolism.

Ectothermia presents certain advantages for the metabolism of "cold-blooded" species. Normally, a reptile has the same temperature as its environment, but it can make its temperature vary, either biologically or behaviorally. Therefore, when swimming, a turtle raises its temperature, making it possible to survive in cold waters. It can also surround itself with a thick layer of fat, which effectively protects it from temperature variations. Finally, the turtle can adopt different behaviors to get cool or warm, both on land and in the sea. For example, it can move toward sunny or sheltered areas or dive down into deep waters. This is why sea turtles can be found in the cold waters of Greenland. The animal maintains an internal temperature of 68°F (20°C) thanks to its thermal inertia, its thick layer of fat, and its intense muscle activity. Evidence indicates

that a sea turtle with stress due to very low temperatures or to forced submergence, as one caught in a fishing net, can employ anaerobic metabolism for a short period of time.

Ectothermia has particularly great advantages in terms of adaptation to varied environments and energy expenditure. It is believed that a turtle of equal weight uses 30 times less energy than a man. Oxygenation in some aquatic species—and especially in the leatherback sea turtle, which is highly pelagic—is done through the skin and the oral, pharyngeal, or cloacal mucous membranes, without returning to the surface, using the small amount of oxygen stored in its lungs, then reducing its metabolism in order to reduce its need for oxygen. Hatchling sea turtles are especially attuned to light and brightness. As they scramble upward through the sand of their egg deposition site, they look around and then crawl rapidly toward the horizon (or the nearest bright lights, which is why subdued lighting on beaches is so vital).

Sea turtles, however, have their preferred climate zones, and depend very closely on the climate and temperature for their reproductive cycle. During their lives, based on their needs, they choose an appropriate environment and temperature, living almost always at their thermal optimum, which makes them privileged among the chelonians.

Unlike land turtles, sea turtles do not hibernate, and while they live primarily in warm waters at relatively constant temperatures, they engage in **permanent activity** without periods of metabolic slowdown. At night, and sometimes during the day, they can be seen sleeping on the surface of the water, or sometimes in underwater caves, wedged between two rocks in order to sleep. They can remain there for several hours.

Little is known of sea turtle **longevity.** It is known that they reach the age of reproductive maturity rather quickly, probably at around six to eight years of age, and that they acquire a large tail very quickly, which makes it possible for them to survive in a hostile universe by protecting them from predators, but their life span is unknown.

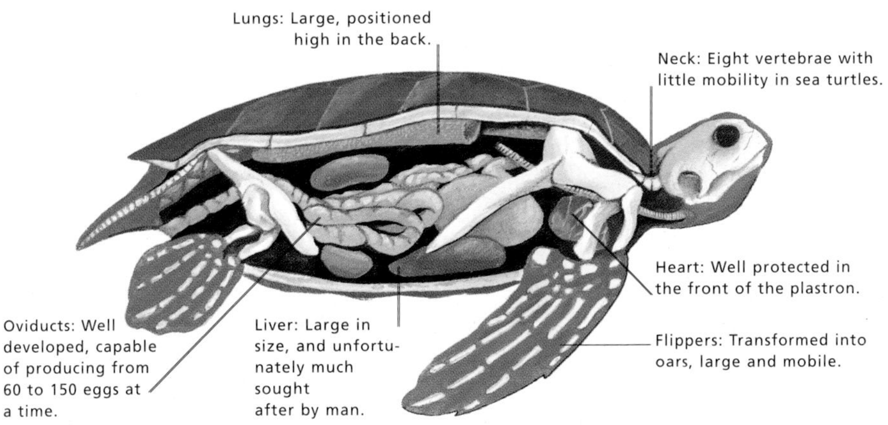

Anatomical cross section of a turtle.

t is assumed that they live at least 30 to ·0 years, short in comparison with the life pan of land turtles, which is 150 years for ome species. In nature, very large sea animals are occasionally seen, but it is difficult o assign them a specific age, as histological tudies do not make it possible to predict age ·eyond 20 years. It is estimated that very arge turtles, such as a leatherback sea turtle veighing 2,095 pounds (950 kg), found dead ·n a beach, must be more than 50 years old.

Behavior and Way of Life

All turtle species have a different way of life, s they are adapted to very dissimilar environments. Sea turtles are less diversified than heir terrestrial or freshwater relatives, but he environment in which they live is relatively uniform.

Mating

Chelonian reproduction is, generally speaking, very similar to that of all vertebrates, vith the intromission of the male organ into the female organ. Moreover, reptiles "invented" the amniotic egg, a hard capsule independent from the external world, which survives by its own means, and incubates in the ground. Because of this requirement, sea turtles, while totally devoted to the aquatic environment, must return several times each year to the perilous natal ground.

For all chelonians, it is the male that has the strong libido, while the female appears to avoid the reproductive act.

Mating of sea turtles can be seen opposite the nesting beaches, where the males wait for the females to return after laying their eggs. Often, first courtship, then mating take place on the surface of the water, as the two animals need to breathe deeply during the act. The male attaches himself to the back of the female with his front claw; his large, strong tail makes it possible for him to hold the female from underneath while his penis penetrates her. This is not a simple action, and gives rise to whirlpools and violent aquatic movements. Sometimes a third animal, and even a fourth, joins in,

there any more beautiful sight than that of two green sea turtles swimming together, the ale on the female's back, in mid-ocean? Occasionally, however, the weight of the male drags e female down to the bottom and drownings have been known to result.

weighing down the couple. The animals occasionally fall gently to the bottom of the water, which may actually cause the female to drown. Occasionally, sea turtles can be seen mating face to face, but this is very rare.

The sperm can remain in the folds of the oviducts, causing ovulation to occur several months and even years after fertilization has taken place.

Egg Laying

After fertilization, the development of the eggs is rather brief—between two and three weeks—then the female has to find a place to lay them. Usually, she returns to the beach where she herself was born, but some choose new beaches. The moment that she leaves the water to drag herself with some difficulty onto the sand of the nesting beach is dependent on hormonal and environmental factors; it is almost always **during the rising tide**, in order to reach the highest part of the beach, and **at night**, perhaps to avoid the daytime heat.

Each turtle species has its method for laying eggs, in regularity, substrata, and methodology. No animal is exactly like another, and significant individual differences can also be seen. The number of eggs per laying depends on the size of the female the leatherback turtle lays the largest numbe of eggs, with seven to eleven clutches laid per year, 100 eggs in each clutch. The eggs c the species weigh approximately 1.8 ounces (50 g) and are approximately 2 inches (5.5 cm) in diameter.

The laying of eggs by sea turtles is more impressive since the females are leaving an environment in which they are at ease—the water—to haul themselves up with difficulty into a hostile world. They must do so quickl in order to avoid dehydration and to quickly return to their preferred environment. If the sun surprises them, if they are blocked by a mass of driftwood, they can lose their lives. Occasionally, the beach is very slanted, or full of obstacles, and the female must travel many feet before finding the line of vegetation the tidewater does not reach. She

Witnessing the laying of eggs by a sea turtle is always a moving moment for the observer, but frontal photographs should be avoided, especially those taken with a flash. It is advisable to wait until the animal is in the egg-laying phase before approaching.

chooses a place free of vegetation, in ground that is soft and slightly damp, so that the hole she digs does not collapse, then she marks off a circular area. She begins to dig the hole itself, throwing the substratum right and left. Her delicate, mobile flippers make precise work possible; phalanges resembling large prehensile hands can be seen moving underneath the skin of the flippers. When the hole is dug—16 inches to 2 feet (40 to 60 cm) deep, according to the species—the turtle rests for a few minutes. Her cloaca dilates, her tail bends toward the bottom of the hole, and she begins to lay her eggs in sudden bursts, breathing heavily with fatigue. When the 50 or 100 eggs are in place, she quickly recovers the hole with her rear flippers, then she turns around in place to camouflage the placement of the eggs and returns as quickly as possible to the sea, where she can breathe easily. The entire process takes no more than an hour and 20 minutes for the Kemp's Ridley and the olive Ridley sea turtle. The latter has an original way of completing her nest. As her carapace has the pronounced shape of a roof, with flat sides, she undulates violently from left to right, like the cover on a pot of boiling water. This packs down the soil and hides the nesting place. Then, very quickly, she turns and escapes to the sea. Among leatherback turtles, on the other hand, the operation lasts for one hour, and the heavy seagoing vessel returns very slowly to the sea, with great strokes of her powerful flippers.

After the first egg laying, a female may return, once, twice, or more, at two- or three-week intervals, to begin again on the same beach. At one time, egg collectors had found a method for predicting the female's return to the beach. When they would find a newly dug nest—upturned sand—they would identify it using a small stick of wood with a string. Every day, they would add a knot to the string and, on the fourteenth day, they would wait on the beach for the female to return. They knew that there was a good possibility that the female would return two or three weeks after her last egg laying.

A camera placed at the bottom of the nest photographed the eggs of a leatherback sea turtle as they emerged. The eggs are spherical and resemble golf balls (approximately 2 inches [50 mm] in diameter).

The eggs vary according to species. Those of land turtles are generally hard and calcified; those of sea turtles are spherical, rather soft, and covered with an aqueous substance that makes them easier to lay and cushions the fall into the deep nest.

Birth

The incubation of the eggs depends on a number of factors, such as their size and number, the depth of the hole and the state of the substratum, the external temperature, the characteristics of the species, and so on. In the 1970s Claude Pieau, a researcher, observed that temperature could change the sex of newborns. In fact, while genetic sex is determined at conception, the incubation temperature during a certain period of embryogenesis—at approximately the third week—can influence the sex, and

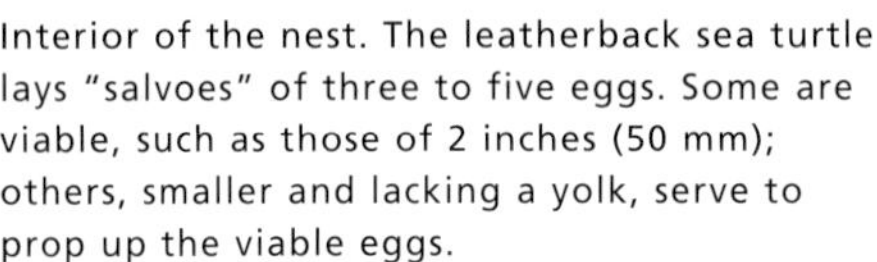

Interior of the nest. The leatherback sea turtle lays "salvoes" of three to five eggs. Some are viable, such as those of 2 inches (50 mm); others, smaller and lacking a yolk, serve to prop up the viable eggs.

Three successive views make it possible to follow the emergence of the young leatherbacks after an average incubation period of 60 days.

produce only males or females. This discovery is fundamentally interesting, but it is also useful for conservation as it makes it possible to produce only males or females, according to the requirements of protection programs.

For sea turtles, incubation lasts between 45 and 70 days, but with exceptions, according to the beach, the climate, and the time of year. During incubation, numerous dangers await the embryos, especially among sea turtles. Predators such as wild dogs or pigs detect the odor of eggs through the ground, or simply by smelling the upturned soil, but burrowing beetles and other small insects—such as ants—can also devour an entire nest of eggs. Finally, the eggs can be carried off by a sudden flood if there are violent storms or if the sea rises abnormally. The ground can then cave in, and at times tourists planting their beach umbrellas or building sand castles have destroyed a nest. Even sadder—females occasionally dig up the eggs of an earlier nesting. This often happens in areas where there are many nests, such as in the Les Hattes in French Guiana, or in Ostional in Costa Rica.

Also, once incubation is over, the young turtle sometimes cannot climb out of the ground, and dies there. This problem only occasionally affects sea turtles, as the sand is moist, and the young turtles are born mature, at the right time, and rapidly. The phenomenon of emerging from a sea turtle

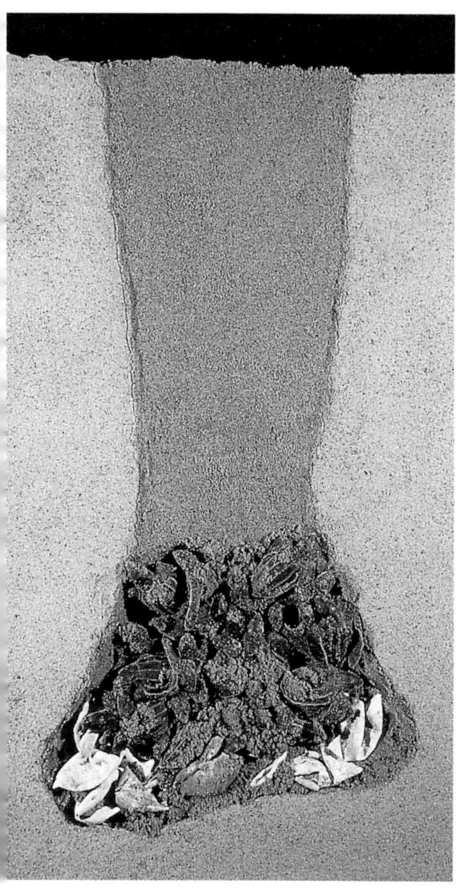

Almost all of the turtles have broken free of their shells, but the process of climbing to the top of the nest has not yet begun.

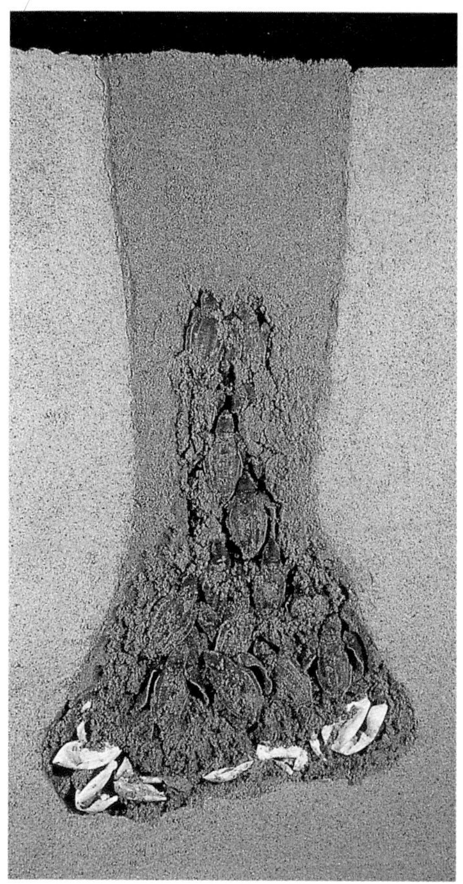

After several hours, the young turtles begin their climb to the top. They all leave at the same time, preferably during the night.

nest remains complex; probably the first ones born are in the middle of the nest, as it is warmer there, but they wait for the emergence of all the others. Once all are born, there is much movement inside the nest that causes the turtles to rise up and, at that moment, they all push at the same time to come out. The sand can be seen to suddenly cave in, with small heads emerging from it. Then 10 or 20 turtles follow and hurry out. In a few minutes, the juveniles head toward the sea, which is the brightest, most brilliant portion of their horizon. As they are quite numerous, they must be born at night, or at nightfall, to limit the risks from predators, but it is not known how they know when to leave the ground. If it is daytime, vultures, wild dogs, pigs, or seabirds that observe them from the sky will quickly devour them; only one or two will escape this massacre. At night, turtles have fewer enemies, at least until they reach the sea, where they must fear carnivorous fish or crabs. A turtle must immediately return to the sea, as it is "programmed" to move its flippers vigorously for at least two or three days, in order to distance itself from the beach and to head toward its feeding grounds. If it is kept in captivity during the first days, it loses the instinct to swim strongly, and when it is returned to the sea it will no longer have the energy to escape and will quickly perish.

Birth is the most crucial and moving moment of life. These eggs placed in an incubator will soon be broken, following 50 to 60 days of incubation—between 77° and 90°F (25° and 32°C)—by the tiny muzzle of a sea turtle, already prepared to face the harsh realities of the ocean.

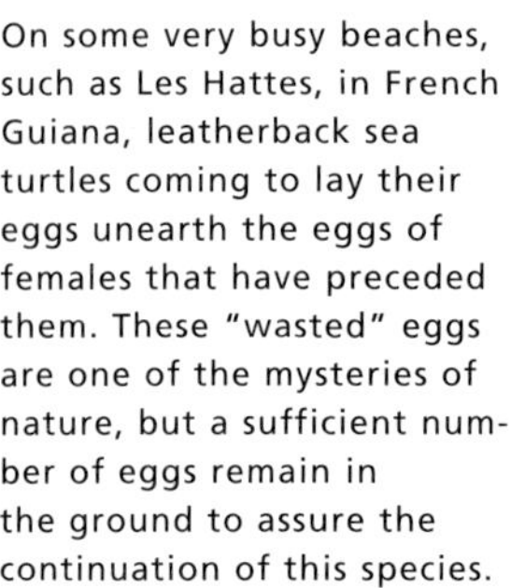

On some very busy beaches, such as Les Hattes, in French Guiana, leatherback sea turtles coming to lay their eggs unearth the eggs of females that have preceded them. These "wasted" eggs are one of the mysteries of nature, but a sufficient number of eggs remain in the ground to assure the continuation of this species.

Crabs, which can weigh up to 6.6 pounds (3 kg), are predators of newly born turtles, quickly gobbling up the fragile juveniles.

Other predators are more insidious, such as the *courtilière,* a small burrowing insect with powerful legs that perforates the eggs and feeds on them.

But when the young leatherback turtle reaches the sea, it is still not out of danger. Silurids, catfish, and sharks all find them delectable.

Be Careful of the Flash!

After four months of effort on the beaches of French Guiana, in collaboration with the scientific team at Yalimapo, and thanks to sophisticated and ingenious equipment, Olivier Grunewald and Bernadette Gilbertas succeeded in photographing leatherback sea turtles in intimate situations. A real challenge, both photographically and zoologically, these photographs made it possible to document the behavior of small turtles as they migrate toward the surface, but also the predation caused by the courtilière and the catfish. Combining esthetics with scientific knowledge, these images, paid for by the World Press and published throughout the world, have greatly contributed toward a better understanding of the species both by scientists and the general public. These photographs were taken under the authorization of the scientific team. Flash photos or the use of powerful lights are strongly discouraged on the beach of Les Hattes, as they disturb the turtles.

Leatherbacks prefer it to be dark at the moment of emergence, so that they will not be seized by predators. The camera flash shows dozens of newborns ready to return to the sea, in French Guiana.

In the mouth of the leatherback sea turtle, there are numerous pilosities resembling thorns. These papillae are rather soft, and can reach 2 inches (5 cm) in length. They are used to facilitate digestion by aiding in swallowing and by preventing the expulsion of solid matter when the turtle ingests jellyfish while diving deep underwater. These pilosities are also used for oxygenating the animal.

Feeding and Growth

In general, land turtles are herbivorous, freshwater turtles carnivorous, and sea turtles eclectic. But there are major differences between the species, often due to the environment in which the animals live. Thus, among sea turtles, some "graze" on coral, which provides them with calcium; others prefer aquatic vegetation, algae, and underwater grasses; and finally, others, more carnivorous, ingest small invertebrates, alevins, and other organic debris floating in the water, fish, or octopus that they can cut apart with their sharp beaks. Leatherback sea turtles prefer jellyfish.

The young feed on the underwater prairies or hidden herbariums, which are not well known; it is not known, for example, where young leatherback turtles spend the first years of their lives. Turtles generally grow slowly and there are major differences between species, according to size. In general, sea turtles grow rapidly, as danger from predators is great in the aquatic environment. Thus, young leatherback turtles, which weigh approximately 1.7 ounces (50 g) at birth, can weigh 4.4 pounds (2 kg) at one year, perhaps 44 pounds (20 kg) at three to four years, and can reach 660 pounds (300 kg) at maturity, in around ten to fourteen years! Other sea turtles also grow very quickly during the first ten years, then their growth rate slows down. Chelonians never completely stop growing. That is how sea turtles are capable of reaching record-breaking weights, such as the leatherback sea turtle

Juveniles of the eight species of sea turtles.

of 2,095 pounds (950 kg) previously mentioned.

Movement and Migration
Sea turtles are the chelonians that move around the most, especially the leatherback sea turtle and the green sea turtle. After leaving the beach where they were born, they travel to the feeding grounds, often unknown. Subadults and adults, they travel the world looking for places to feed, then for places to reproduce and lay their eggs. Their sense of direction is highly developed; some turtles have been fitted with tracking devices in order to follow their migration. They often follow the underwater currents, but little is known of the reasons for their movement—and why shouldn't they keep this a secret?

Despite their skill at navigating the waters of the world, sea turtles turn up in unexpected places. Live and often stranded loggerhead turtles have been found along the European coast or near Great Britain. These turtles are thought to have originated in North America, and to have been transported by the North Atlantic current and the Gulf Stream.

Differentiation

There are eight sea turtle species in the world, which is very few in comparison with the 260 species of chelonians; seven are part of the Cheloniidae family and have a bony carapace; the eighth, the leatherback sea turtle, is the sole representative of the Dermochelyidae family and, as its name indicates, is covered with a thick coat of leather. All are characterized by front limbs in the form of large flat flippers, which make rapid swimming possible, and by rear racket-shaped flippers, which serve primarily for orientation. Speeds of 17 mph (27 km) have been noted in sea turtles, with some reaching 22 mph (35 km), which is remarkable in an environment as dense as the sea. Yet this streamlining of a sea turtle means it has lost the ability to retract its head and appendages into its shell for protection. Each species is distinguished from the others by the shape of the carapace and the number or the form of the scutes on the head and on the back. In the species descriptions, we shall specify these differences, which are important in order to recognize each animal, and it will also be necessary to refer to the drawings.

The eight existing species are:

– *Chelonia mydas,* perhaps the most widely distributed, the best known, and also the most exploited, called the green sea turtle because of the color of its fat, and not that of its shell, which is often more brown or beige than green. It is found in almost all the oceans of the world.

– *Chelonia agassizii* is very similar to the preceding species and is found only in the western part of North and South America. It is called the black sea turtle.

– *Caretta caretta* is also a sea turtle known since antiquity, called the loggerhead sea turtle. It frequents the same waters as the green sea turtle.

– Another species known and exploited by man is the *hawksbill sea turtle,* not to be confused with the loggerhead: *Eretmochelys imbricata.* Its overlapping scutes have given it its name—and its problems. It is not a great sea traveler and prefers to stay close to the shore, throughout the equatorial and tropical parts of the oceans.

– Two smaller, more rare, and more endangered species are the olive *Ridley sea turtle, Lepidochelys olivacea,* and the *Kemp's Ridley sea turtle, Lepidochelys kempii.* The latter is the smallest of the sea turtles, and is also the one most reduced in number. It is found only in the waters of the eastern part of the United States and Mexico, in the North Atlantic, and in the western part of Europe. This turtle, coastal by nature and carnivorous, has had its numbers fall dangerously low, and has had its nesting grounds shrink. All available methods are currently being used to avoid extinction, and that is why we have voluntarily decided not to provide any information on the nesting sites of the Kemp's Ridley sea turtle, which requires the greatest tranquility in order to reproduce.

– *Natator depressus,* another species similar to the green sea turtle, is found only in Australian waters, except in the southern part of the continent. Its popular name is the *flatback sea turtle.*

– Finally, the "star" among sea turtles, *Dermochelys coriacea,* or the leatherback sea turtle, the heaviest, the most migratory, the most widely distributed, the most atypical, and perhaps the most beautiful of all. These are seen as far north as Alaska and as far south as the tip of Africa. The order chosen in the pages that follow is that of the systematic classification.

These eight chelonians of the high seas, adapted to the marine environment only in the last 80 years, are your nocturnal companions along the beaches of the world; it is up to you to admire their nobility and their lightness, their obstinacy and their beauty. You can see them gasping and heavy at the moment of egg laying, or rapid and airborne during their underwater journeys. For herpetologists, these are the uncontested stars of the vast oceans.

'he Kemp's Ridley sea turtle *(Lepidochelys kempii)* is the rarest and most retiring of all sea urtles. It does not exceed 99 pounds (45 kg), with a grayish carapace that is often more wide han long and appears higher, like a bump, toward the front of the back. Its last sanctuary, in he Gulf of Mexico, has given cause for hope that its numbers will increase; eggs have been noved there to recreate populations on nonpopulated beaches and new females have been dentified. If the protective measures—no drift nets, protection of beaches, and so on—are ffective, there is hope this species can be saved.

TURTLES AND MAN

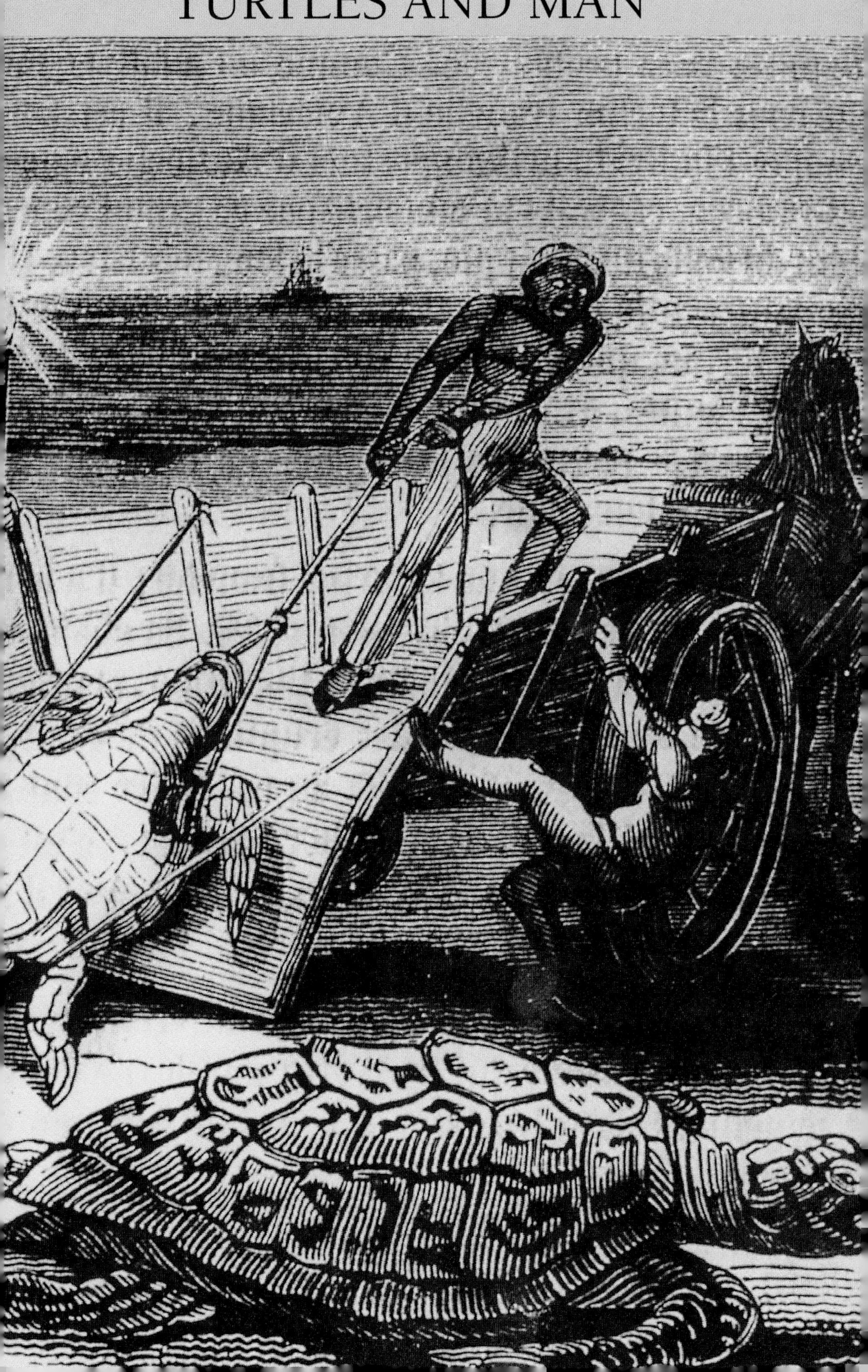

An Unloved Creature

Turtles have been known to man for thousands of years, and have, unfortunately, often ended up on his plate.

Easy to capture, offering varied and diverse products, believed not to suffer—a turtle does not cry and does not show obvious pain, according to those who do not want to see it—turtles have always been man's companions and laughingstocks. Many species have even been made extinct by man; certain turtles from the Mascareignes, for example, were wiped out in three centuries, but much earlier, Asian species had already become extinct as a result of human exploitation. About 5,000 years ago, in China, the plastron of certain species were used to tell the future; tens of thousands of them have been exhumed during archaeological digs. The remains of turtles have also been found in the caves of our ancestors, as at Terra-Amata, near Nice.

Man, fascinated by the longevity and exceptional fertility of the turtle, has always had mixed feelings of veneration and alimentary lust for it. The Dogons, for example, saw it as a mediator between the gods and the village chief, which did not prevent them from dismembering it alive and eating it in order to benefit from its attributes. In China people still drink the blood of soft-shelled turtles for energy prior to races and games. In India the turtle, one of the avatars of Vishnu, also holds up the world; in the East it is also the symbol of longevity and fertility; and among Native Americans it is one of the basic totems of the creation of the universe. In Greece it represented, along with the dolphin, the god Poseidon. In our own culture, the turtle is supposed to represent wisdom. We recognize the turtle's slow and deliberate nature when we recount Aesop's story about the tortoise and the hare.

But the turtle has suffered because it is edible from the end of the tail to the end of its horny beak. Everything in the turtle can be eaten, or used, which earned the green sea turtle, *Chelonia mydas*, for example, the name "pig of the sea": meat, eggs, fat, shells, leather. Not so long ago, in Rèunion, turtle steaks were sold on a farm. The liver is considered to be a delicacy, and the eggs have always been eaten in such countries as Costa Rica and India. These eggs are unusual, as the white does not coagulate. In South America, oil was extracted from turtle fat that was highly valued for lighting lamps as well as for consumption. Boxes and musical instruments were made from the carapace. In fact, Mercury may have invented the lute by using the carapace and the entrails of a turtle. Its dried penis was long considered an aphrodisiac.

The great turtle massacres date back to the sixteenth through the nineteenth centuries, when pirates, navigators, and whalers traveled the high seas, collecting everything possible. These pirates, our ancestors, collected enormous numbers of turtles in the Indian Ocean and the Antilles, sending millions of them back to Europe, where they ended up in turtle soup. They were also used on boats as meat. They were able to survive for long periods of time without food and water, and were killed during the voyage to feed the crew. Thus, it was the sea turtle that paid the highest price, especially the green sea turtle. More than 100 million females were certainly hunted and captured on the nesting beaches over the course of three centuries. Turned on their backs, attached by their flippers with a cable, they were subjected to neglect and abuse by the crew, storms, and burning sun, ending up cut to pieces—while still alive, of course—in the pots of English or American ships. Some marine species have almost disappeared, and one of them, the Kemp's Ridley sea turtle, is on the brink of extinction.

Silver medallions, struck in ancient Greece, often showed sea turtles, symbolizing Poseidon (from top to bottom, medallions from Egine, ca. 560 B.C. and ca. 470–450 B.C., Cretan medallion from the fourth or fifth century B.C.)

Today, the status of the turtles has changed. Although still eaten in Asia, in South America, and occasionally in some African countries, the land turtle has suddenly taken on the image of an easygoing animal, cleaner of snails, and garden ornament. Unfortunately, this transformation threatens it all the more, as a result of the kinds of traffic to which it is subjected. Sea turtles, on the other hand, have not had been subject to this new fashion for pet reptiles; moreover, they do not do well in captivity, and in aquaria where some are kept, they rarely live beyond 15 years. The leatherback sea turtle, for example, does not tolerate being contained in a closed environment. More obstinate than the others, it bangs its head against the walls of its glass cage and refuses to eat. It is not known how this turtle grows, how it survives, or how it eats, but, is it not made, like the great cetaceans, for the open seas and freedom?

Dangers and Conservation

As has been seen, many dangers threaten turtles, which are slow animals without defenses, but a distinction must be made between natural dangers, which have never threatened the survival of species, and dangers from man, which are much more destructive. Sea turtles are all protected today and are included in Appendix I of CITES (an international organization for the regulation of animal commerce). However, they are still collected in Asia and in Polynesia, and their eggs are also used in some Central American and African countries. Indirectly, they suffer from pollution of the seas, often suffocating in drift nets. Finally, the disturbance or the urbanization of nesting beaches keeps females away from those beaches and compromises the survival of some populations, such as those in the Gulf of Mexico or Turkey. On some beaches, hotels and houses that are illuminated at night disturb the females, and disorient the hatchlings at the moment of birth.

For the last 50 years, more and more herpetologists and scientists have been concerned with the conservation of land, freshwater, and sea turtles. Books have been published and organizations have come to their aid. Finally, centers of protection or study have been created throughout the world, and ranching has made reintroduction possible. Head-start programs provide safe incubation for eggs from threatened or partially destroyed nests. Hatchlings are housed and fed until they grow just past the "one- bite-size" stage, then released at the original nest site. Conservation is the most difficult to implement for sea turtles, as it requires problems to be treated more globally, sea turtles being world citizens. It is not by protecting a single beach, or a small maritime zone, that these migratory animals will be saved. Nesting beaches must be monitored, the use of drift nets limited—or special pockets known as TED (Turtle Exclusion Device) used, which make it possible for turtles and other large animals to escape through the back of the net—eggs placed in protected enclosures, the use of tortoiseshell or turtle flesh prohibited, tourists educated not to buy these animals, and sometimes reintroductions, by means of eggs transported from one zone to another, as in the Gulf of Mexico, must take place. The protection of sea turtles, therefore, is dependent on the general ecology of our planet. By protecting the sea, the turtles are protected.

On-site observation may be a good addition to conservation, and it is up to the general public today, to those who love turtles and observe them on the beaches, to participate in their protection and to provide them with moral or financial support. It is also by means of education, such as through this book, that turtles will be viewed as they should be—as animals that are very ancient and very threatened, whose environment must be preserved, and that are part of the inheritance of all of us.

In fact, there are two opposing currents: the urban and economic development of the planet, and the imperative need to protect disappearing fauna and flora. Ecotourism may be a good link between economics and conservation. To see turtles on nesting beaches can only serve to educate. It can help turtles to become respected and to become better known. They have ceased to be consumable products, but they must become free animals, without the need to fear human activities.

And above all, remember: **turtle-based products should not be purchased for any reason whatsoever,** whether it is for the famous turtle soup, or articles made from tortoiseshell, or as trophies.

The Green Sea Turtle

(*Chelonia mydas*)
FRENCH: tortue franche, tortue verte
SPANISH: tortuga verde

32

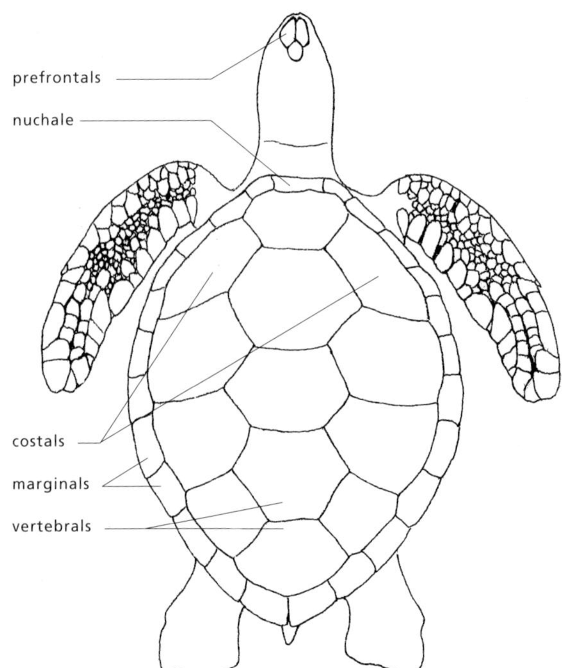

Drawing indicating differentiation of *Chelonia mydas:*
- Nuchal does not touch the first costals.
- Head has only a single pair of prefrontals.
- Muzzle is rounded.

Description

Measurements: adult female between 31.5 inches (80 cm) and 51 inches (130 cm) (length of the back).

Average weight: 352 to 550 pounds (160 to 250 kg); weights of 870 pounds (400 kg) have been observed.

This is the largest of the seven species having a carapace.

The green sea turtle has a cordiform (heart-shaped) **carapace** with juxtaposed horny plates. The nuchal shell is not in contact with the first lateral costals, and there are four pairs of costal shells on the back. The **back** is slightly rounded in the front, and narrower in the back; it is brownish, occasionally olive green or gray, marked by lighter streaks, especially in the young. The seams of the plates form light yellow lines on the marbled or olive green of the animal. It has well-rounded marginals, giving the species a very round shape resembling that of a pebble.

It has a yellowish white **plastron**, rather wide, occasionally with two longitudinal keels in adults, which are much more visible in young individuals. There are four pairs of inframarginal plates on each side, rather rigid.

The **head** is easily recognizable, rather small, with a short, round muzzle and two prefrontal scutes, separated from a broad parietal front by a rather small frontal scute. It has a very strong serrated beak. The scutes are underlined in yellow on a beige, brown, or olive green background. The eyes are very large, which gives this animal an air of watchfulness.

The **flippers** are gray on top, sometimes green with darker scutes, rather wide, with lighter edges, cream or yellow, and yellowish underneath. Well adapted for swimming and wide, the flippers are very flexible in back, and more delicate in front, with a single claw. The animal has soft, regular skin, like supple leather. Males have a very long, wide, prehensile tail, with a keratinized end. Their claws are more developed than in the female, which has shorter, more delicate tails.

A new and distressing development in green turtles are large skin tumors, called fibropapillomas, which can obscure vision and mobility. There is no known cause and no known cure.

Distribution

This turtle is in all waters where the temperature exceeds 68°F (20°C)—the Atlantic, Mediterranean, and Pacific, except for the east coast of America where is it replaced by its conspecific, *Cheloniamydas agassizii*—but no further south than Tasmania, and no further north than the British Isles. It is found in varied environments, depending on its age, or on its food or reproductive needs. During the early years, it frequents still unknown places, then grasslands during the growing period of young adults, and finally reproduction areas. Each year they gather in large groups to nest; perhaps one of the best known nesting sites is that on Ascension Island. Nesting sites can be several thousand miles away from feeding sites. Sea turtles, in general, are not gregarious, and can travel to various distant sites and cross them; thus they can be found in several seas, several nesting beaches, and several migratory circuits. There has been no long-term monitoring of these animals.

Diet

Carnivorous in their youth—small invertebrates, fish eggs, mollusks, and jellyfish—then omnivorous. They frequent underwater prairies, where they can be found in significant numbers in certain regions. The digestion of cellulose from aquatic plants by the microflora in their intestines is comparable to that of land ruminants. The weak nutritional value of algae and aquatic plants explains the relatively slow growth rate of this species, along with its late maturity. However, the diet is more omnivorous than it appears; by ingesting vegetation, the turtles also ingest small underwater fauna such as crustaceans, mollusks, jellyfish, and sponges.

Close-up of the head of a green sea turtle showing the frontal and prefrontal scutes of this species. These horny plates offer excellent protection against external dangers.

This species is alone among sea turtles in occasionally insulating itself in the sand, for the purpose of regulating body temperature. As a result, this is the only species in which the presence of males outside of the water has occasionally, but very rarely, been noted. It is believed that this practice may be linked with the absorption of ultraviolet rays that are necessary for fixing calcium and vitamins, specifically vitamin D, which are lacking in its diet.

Mating

Sexual maturity is reached at between 8 and 15 years. It is believed that the green sea turtle is receptive only on certain days, and probably when she is laying eggs. Some males, more enterprising and aggressive than others, demonstrate a dominating behavior. The female occasionally refuses to mate, in which case she bites the male or holds herself vertically to prevent coupling. During courtship, the male delicately nibbles the neck and shoulders of his partner, which are her most sensitive parts. Finally, if the female is receptive, he attaches himself to her sides with his powerful claws. He uses his rear flippers to direct his tail and his penis toward the female's cloaca. Mating can take place over the course of several hours, both on the surface and underwater, and occasionally in deep water. During surface mating, the male's "tenderness" is amazing, with him gently placing his front flippers on the back or the head of the female. These moments of intimacy can be observed by visitors traveling noiselessly in a rowboat in the waters close to the nesting areas, where the males gather to await the return of the females.

Males gather at these beaches because they have a better chance of finding a female. Some females may lay as many as 11 clutches a season.

Egg Laying

Females have a spermateca that receives and stores sperm, and a single mating makes it possible for all their eggs to be fertilized during one, or even several seasons. Some of the eggs develop in one or two oviducts, and when the first eggs are mature, they are laid, while the second, smaller ones, grow in turn. Egg laying takes place in 15-day intervals. Green sea turtles frequent many beaches: Costa Rica, French Guiana, Suriname, Mexico, Ascension Islands, Trinity, Cape Verde, Bermuda, Cayman Islands, Cuba, and Brazil. In the Caribbean Islands, egg laying takes place from March to October, particularly in May–June, on Ascension Day, from December to July, with February–April the peak. In the Mediterranean it is especially frequent in the east—Turkey, Cyprus, Israel, Greece—but some recent observations in Spain, Italy, and France make it possible to suppose that formerly this species came to nest more often on these coasts.

The green sea turtle uses its forward flippers first to mark off the egg-laying area, and digs an initial hole, as wide as its body, then the nest itself with its rear flippers, for approximately one-half hour, in the slightly damp ground of an area out of the reach of high waters. The hole is between 12 and 17 inches (30 to 50 cm) wide, and wider on the bottom, in the form of a bottle. Once the nest chamber has been dug, the female will position her hind flippers over the chamber as she lays her eggs. The eggs, 1.8 inches (45 mm) in diameter, round, with a supple and wrinkled membrane, numbering approximately 100, are ejected two or three at a time, with a discharge of mucus. Then the female covers up the nest, first by an alternating movement of the rear flippers, then by broad jets of sand, using the front flippers by turning around and around and flattening the sand with her carapace. The entire process, rather rapid, lasts an average of one and a half hours. Occasionally, if there is driftwood blocking the beach, egg laying can take twice as long, and sometimes the animal can get stuck there and die. A sea turtle, in fact, has enormous difficulty in moving backward, as the conformation of its flippers does not permit an inverse movement of its four limbs.

Incubation lasts between 48 and 74 days, according to the ground temperature and the general climate. The hatchlings have a dark carapace with marginals bordered in white, like the edges of the flippers. Their plastron and the underside of the flippers are white spotted with black. Subadults have a more colorful carapace, beginning as reddish brown or mahogany, always with yellow lines, then becoming more brown or dark green, and more uniform in color, losing the earlier light streaks.

Conservation

This was the most exploited of the sea turtles, and its name "pig of the seas" was unfortunately largely merited. Its shell is less valued than that of the hawksbill sea turtle, but it was also sometimes used. It is from its cartilage, its flesh, and its fat that, formerly, the famous turtle soup was made. Before sea turtles became protected, canned green turtle soup was a popular tourist souvenir from island countries. Its skin also provided a rather convenient leather, and its fat was used for multiple purposes such as lighting, food, and salves. The male's penis was also much prized, and many turtles ended up as trophies.

This turtle is still exploited. There are a few ranches on the Cayman Islands or in Réunion. It is, in fact, easy to breed, and it withstands captivity rather well. Having a great deal of fat, it can grow quickly, and at three years of age can weigh some 89 pounds (40 kg). Today, it suffers from ocean pollution—tar, plastic bags, and so on—and the use of drift nets. While its numbers are still large, many decades will be needed to return to former levels.

Fortunately, monitored reserves have been established in Sri Lanka and in Brazil, and other initiatives are also worth noting. In the mid 1970s, Caretta Research, Inc., aided by the Florida Department of Natural Resources, head-started dozens of hatchling green turtles on Sanibel Island. The young turtles, hale and hearty after eight to ten months of captivity and a steady diet, were released into the Gulf of Mexico. None of the tagged turtles have been recovered—which only means they have not washed ashore as carcasses or been recorded by one of the nesting monitors at Sanibel. In Cyprus—there are, according to some sources, only 500 green sea turtles in the Mediterranean—a team of volunteers has formed around Andreas Pistentis, a well-known ecologist, to protect nesting sites on the Lara beach. The placement in monitored enclosures of a portion of the first nestings on the beach make it possible to save between 8,000 and 10,000 hatchlings a year. On board a rapid launch, Pistentis also monitors the fishing nets; when a turtle is trapped in one of them, he returns it to the sea, thereby preventing it from ending up in a restaurant kitchen.

For the green sea turtle, the fight for survival continues in certain areas of the world, namely, the Indonesian coasts. In Tanjung Benoa (Bali), there has always been the custom of sacrificing 30 green sea turtles a week for rituals that no longer have anything to do with religion. Thus, when a young couple gets married, or when a dignitary wishes to make a sacrifice to the gods or to receive a pardon for an offense against some divinity, he buys a turtle enclosed in the bamboo prisons of Benoe, and it is immolated in the name of sacrosanct traditions. The sight of these noble animals attached by the front flippers with a metal wire, laboring and gasping in one foot of dirty water waiting for the sacrifice, is depressing. They die little by little, without food and in overwhelming heat, then are sold to butchers who cut them into steaks. This slaughter should take place between 2:00 and 3:00 in the morning, according to the principles of the adat, the local religious tradition; the turtles are, however, killed during the day, like ordinary animals at the butcher.

Green sea turtle equipped with a tracking device. Each time the turtle returns to the surface to breathe, the device emits a radio signal in the direction of a satellite. The smallest movement is thus recorded.

Observation Site

Costa Rica: Tortuguero National Park

Costa Rica has, in recent years, acquired the reputation for being one of the major sites of nature tourism in Central America; nature conservation receives more attention there than in the majority of other countries in this region, and the parks and reserves in Costa Rica are often extremely well managed. Green tourism has, moreover, become one of the main national resources of this small country.

Regarding sea turtles, Costa Rica plays a major role in tropical America. Six species frequent its waters, either permanently or during certain times of the year, and four species come to nest there, either on the Atlantic or the Pacific coasts or on both. The green sea turtle is perhaps the most frequent, while the hawksbill sea turtle, the loggerhead sea turtle, the olive Ridley sea turtle, the black sea turtle, and the leatherback sea turtle are also well-represented.

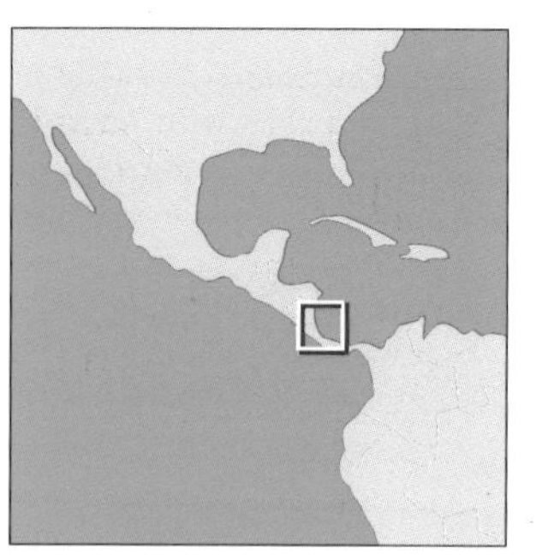

As in the majority of Latin American countries, significant massacres of sea turtles took place in the past, but today, these reptiles are well protected here. The conservation measures adopted have attempted, in fact, to take into account the interests of local populations, which in the long term offer a good guarantee of success.

Various national parks or natural reserves have been created primarily in the context of the conservation of sea turtles. This is the case with the Tortuguero National Park, the Ostional animal refuge, and the Santa Rosa National Park. Other protected sites have also contributed to the conservation of sea turtles, even if it was not initially their principal objective.

Tortuguero National Park is located on the Atlantic (east) coast of Costa Rica, in the north of the country. It covers more than 49,400 acres (20,000 ha) of forest and 123,500 acres (50,000 ha) of sea with

22 miles (35 km) of beach. It is one of the most important natural sites in the country, but it is increasingly subject to human pressure. At present, it is a veritable "island" of nature surrounded by human establishments and plantations—banana, among others—bordering the forest.

Fauna and Flora

Sea turtles, of course, constitute the park's principal attraction, and they give the park its name: *tortuguero,* "place of turtles."

Among the hundreds of species that can be observed in the park, and primarily along the coast, there are frigate birds, terns, sandpipers, herons, and others.

Reptiles are also well represented there; in addition to caimans and crocodiles, there are numerous species of snakes, including the dreaded fer-de-lance or spearhead, as well as the green iguana, in which the males are identifiable during periods of reproduction by their bright costume of green and orange. More than 50 species of amphibians have also been identified in the park, including various species of poison dart frogs or dendrobates (small tropical American frogs) in shimmering or brilliant colors. Seven species of freshwater turtles frequent the forest.

A midnight walk in the woods will reveal dozens of kinds of ornate and beautiful insects, from the sleeping morpho butterfly to the pink and yellow thorny katydid. Fish-eating bats grab their prey from shallow pools near the water's edge. Other mammals are also present, although they are generally more difficult to observe due to the closed nature of the environment, their generally nocturnal habits, and their normal timidity. All three species of primates present in Costa Rica, the white-faced capuchin, the howling monkey, and the spider monkey, can occasionally be seen in the forest canopy, as can sloths at times. Tapirs, peccaries, and several species of cats are also part of the park's fauna, but these animals are rarely seen by visitors.

The profusion of vegetation in the park is also remarkable, with several thousand plants already identified, among which there are almost 500 kinds of tropical trees.

Tortuguero National Park is reached by a network of canals that crisscross the lush tropical forest.

The green iguana *(Iguana iguana)* is one of the most spectacular reptiles of tropical America.

Observation

Tortuguero National Park can be considered one of the best places for the observation of sea turtles in Central America. The new visitor's center serves both as a hospitality and educational site for the park. It is currently the principal reproduction site for the green sea turtle in the Caribbean. Females arrive from the Mosquito Coast, northeast of Nicaragua, as has been demonstrated by the actual marking of these animals.

The population of these turtles has experienced an alarming decline: 20 years ago, the number of females arriving each year to nest in Tortuguero had declined to approximately 3,000. Since the beginning of the 1990s, however, thanks to effective protective measures, these numbers have risen to more than 15,000. The conservation of green sea turtles in Tortuguera has thus often been cited as an example, and serves as a model for a number of other conservation projects in Central America and the Caribbean Islands.

Sporadic egg laying by green sea turtles takes place almost throughout the entire year, but the peak season is between May and July. Several hundred green sea turtles can leave the sea each night to dig their nests in the sand of the beaches of Tortuguera and vicinity.

It is possible to observe these egg layings—approximately one turtle every five minutes. Theoretically, all visitors must be accompanied by an official park guard who can provide interesting information on the biology of the turtles and on the success of conservation measures in effect on site for several decades. The use of lights, even flashlights, and photographic flashes or projectors (video cameras) are prohibited on the beach at night, in order not to disturb the females laying their eggs.

The leatherback sea turtle frequents these beaches in significant numbers, without reaching the density of the green sea turtle. The best time of year to observe them is primarily from April to May. Loggerhead or

Archie Carr, the Forerunner

In the 1950s few naturalists were interested in turtles. The first herpetologist to concern himself with the fate of sea turtles, and with their often conflictual relationships with man, was Archie Carr, an American biologist who is considered the father of chelonian conservation. He discovered many nesting sites, such as Tortuguero, and his many articles and works did much for the understanding and protection of these reptiles. He also trained or inspired many specialists such as Peter Pritchard, and thanks to him, in 1954, the first world center for sea turtle research was established in Tortuguero, today managed by the Caribbean Conservation Corporation (CCC). The harvesting of eggs by villagers is of little importance here, as Tortuguero is a minuscule village, and the closest city, Limón, is 50 miles (80 km) away. However, at night, there have been seen in central Limón collectors transporting still-living green sea turtles, captured, perhaps, on the beaches in the south of Costa Rica.

Archie Carr today would find the beach at Tortuguero similar to the one he knew in 1954, as few tourists visit this distant location and the site has retained its wild and natural aspect, to the great advantage of the turtles.

hawksbill sea turtles also lay their eggs on the beaches of the national park, primarily between March and October, but never in significant numbers.

It is often possible to see sea turtles in the ocean during the main nesting period; these are primarily females waiting in the nearby coastal waters for the optimum conditions to emerge from the water. Mating can also be observed taking place several feet from the beach. Often, turtles that are late can be seen in the early hours of the morning on the beach, but it is rare for egg laying to take place during the day.

PRACTICAL INFORMATION

July and August are the best months to observe the green sea turtle.

TRANSPORTATION

■ **BY PLANE.** The airport in San José, capital of the country, is connected to several U.S. cities by regular flights.

■ **BY BUS.** The closest locality is Moin, also one of the principal departure points for boats providing the link with the national park; arrival by sea is not advised due to the very heavy seas in this area. The city is linked to San José by daily bus service—four to five hours of travel. The visitor in a hurry, or with greater means, can rent a vehicle in San José.

■ **BY BOAT.** The park is located in an area for which access is rather difficult; the last part of the trip to the national park is done by boat. Regular service makes it possible to reach Tortuguero in several hours. The trip through the "canals" surrounded by forest is quite pleasant.

■ **BY SMALL CARRIER.** The quickest way, but the least ecological and the most expensive, is to charter a small plane in San José. A landing strip, built on the edge of the beach for the needs of the park, is open to visitors.

■ **BY GUIDED TOUR.** For those with only a limited amount of time, the simplest way is to sign up for a guided tour; many travel agencies offer excursions to Tortuguero, leaving from San José or Puerto Limón. Plan on at least two days—day trips devote too much time for travel.

ACCOMMODATIONS

It is possible to camp in the immediate vicinity of the park's administrative center; there are rudimentary facilities, but toilets and drinkable water are available.

At the south of the park, the small village of Tortuguero offers various lodging possibilities at very reasonable prices (basic comfort). Small stores sell necessities.

Several lodges have been opened along the edges of the park, north of the village. The majority of people visiting the park on a guided tour spend the night in one of these establishments that have superior comfort, but are more expensive.

The research station run by the CCC, an American-Costa Rican nongovernmental agency primarily concerned with the conservation of sea turtles in Costa Rica, accepts visitors who can demonstrate a specific interest in nature; there is a common dormitory at the research station. Interested individuals should write directly to this organization (Apartado 246-2050, San Pedro, San José; tel.: 224-9215; fax: 225-7516).

CLIMATE

It is hot and humid with 197 inches (5,000 mm) of rain in this region throughout the year—the rainiest months are February and March—that saturate the air with humidity. Most storms are of short duration and take place at the end of the day. Temperatures range from 77° to 86°F (25° to 30°C) during the day; there is little change at night.

TRAVEL CONDITIONS

Permission to enter the park is obtained at the Tortuguero administrative center at the southern entrance, in a place called Estacion de Cuatro Esquinas. Various excursions on foot, by boat, motorboat, or canoe, during the day or at night, with nature guides, are organized, and information is available in the village. There is a small information station, including an exhibit, in the village of Tortuguero.

During the peak nesting season for turtles (July–August), it is possible to participate in scientific research projects concerned with these animals. Stays last two weeks and are paid. Write to the Caribbean Conservation Corporation, 4424 NW 13th Street, Suite 1-A, Gainesville, Florida 32609. Tel.: 1-352-373-6441; Fax: 1-352-375-2449.

Observation Site

Sultanate of Oman: Ra's al Hadd

The Sultanate of Oman remains one of the least-known countries on the Arabian peninsula, perhaps in the entire world. Completely closed off for decades, Oman in fact remained inaccessible for the majority of foreigners until very recently. Among specialists, however, this magnificent country has earned the perfectly justified reputation for being the leader in the Arab world in matters of wild animal conservation. While the best-known animal preservation campaigns—conducted under the personal impetus of the current sultan Abou-bin-Said—concern the Arabian oryx and the great cetaceans, sea turtles have also benefited from intense conservation measures for more than ten years. As in some other Arab countries, the ruler's word is the law, and the legal processes are different from those we are accustomed to.

Oman occupies a strategic position for sea turtles in the Indian Ocean. Five species, in fact, frequent, more or less intensively, its waters and its beaches, either permanently or during particular times of the year. The green sea turtle is the most abundant; it can be found in significant concentrations—occasionally up to several thousand animals—on the immense marine grasslands that stretch out along the east coast of Oman, and several tens of thousands of these turtles also use its beaches for nesting.

As for the loggerhead sea turtle, almost 30,000 females dig their nests annually on the single island of Masirah, located a short distance from the shore, with others regularly visiting the beaches in the south (Dhofar region).

The olive Ridley sea turtle regularly nests along Omani shores, but in a dispersed fashion and never in significant numbers—several hundred individuals per year. Several hundred hawskbill sea turtles come to nest each year on the beaches of the Daymaniyat Islands, off the coast. The enormous leatherback sea turtle is regularly found in the waters of the sultanate, where it is known to feed at certain times of the year, but no recent case is known of this species nesting on the shores of the country.

Today, sea turtles and their principal nesting sites are completely protected by law in Oman. The most important sites in the country have been elevated to the rank of natural reserves; this is specifically the case with the beaches at Ra's al Hadd. Widespread education campaigns are continuously underway with coastal populations, particularly

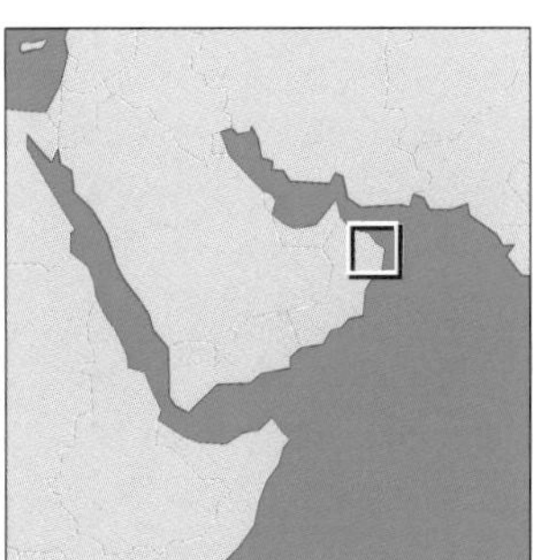

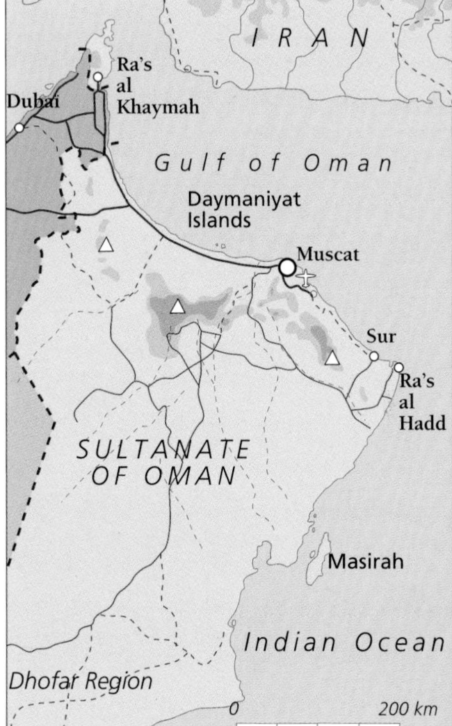

directed toward local fishermen. The fact that no large-scale industrial fishing activity takes place in the coastal waters of the Sultanate of Oman also contributes to the *de facto* protection of the sea turtles.

Ra's al Hadd is the most eastern point on the Omani coast, which, at this point, ends in a small cape heading into the Sea of Oman to turn toward the south and the west as far as the border with neighboring Yemen. The reserve is located at the foot of an imposing group of mountains that separates the coastal band of northern Oman from the high desert plateaus of the interior, approximately 112 miles (180 km) from the capital, Muscat.

Fauna and Flora

The Ra's al Hadd region is one of Oman's numerous desert areas. The arid mountains jut directly into the sea, and vegetation is rare. Only a few villages, none of significant size, are sprinkled along the coast. The inhabitants live almost solely from ocean resources.

The biological poverty of the environment, which is surprising in its beauty, explains why fauna are rare. Insects and reptiles represent the majority of the species present; birds that can be observed on the beaches and the immediate vicinity belong for the most part to marine species, while certain species of passerines such as larks, raptors, goshawks, and falcons, adapted to arid conditions can also be seen in Ra's al Hadd.

Mammals are not, however, totally absent; rodents typical of the desert expanses of the Arabian peninsula (jerboas) manage to survive in the difficult rocky environment, and several species of predators also make more or less regular incursions there such as golden jackals, striped hyenas, and Arabian wolves. The latter even specialize in certain places in the pillage of sea turtle nests during the egg-laying season. These animals are, however, basically nocturnal, and remain very timid. The great predators are in fact persecuted by the local populations, in spite of education efforts on the part of the authorities, so it is exceptional to be able to observe them.

The entrance to Ra's al Hadd (Oman); at the gates of the desert, a paradise for turtles.

Fishing is still practiced on a small scale by most fishermen in Oman.

The natural environment of the Ra's al Hadd is one of great beauty with large abrupt cliffs and rocky outcroppings alternating with long sandy beaches, behind which rise hills of brown, gray, ocher, mauve, and red rocks.

If you visit this area and enjoy swimming, take snorkel and mask with you; the waters teem with a seemingly endless variety of colorful fish. Sea snakes may also be observed, if you're lucky. These venomous snakes live entirely at sea and present danger only to their prey, fish.

Observation

The observation of sea turtles can take place here under very good conditions. During the best season, the summer, the concentrations of green sea turtles coming to dig their nests are often remarkable; some 20,000 green sea turtles nest each year in Oman, of which 6,000 to 13,000, depending on the year, come to the beaches of the Ra's al Hadd area.

The high season for egg laying varies from one species to another—hawksbill turtles are the most numerous in April, loggerhead sea turtles in June, and green sea turtles in July–August; however, egg laying takes place throughout the year on the beaches of Oman.

Visitors must be accompanied by a guide connected with the reserve; they are not very numerous as of this date and are brought in small groups as soon as the guides have

A green sea turtle rushes to return to the sea at daybreak to escape the hot sun (Oman). Almost 20,000 of them arrive each year to lay their eggs on the country's beaches.

identified turtles leaving the sea to dig their nests and lay eggs. While not all guides speak fluent English, their enthusiasm is sufficient to make the visit very interesting. Only the guides are permitted to use sources of light on the beach during the night.

In high season, green sea turtles are still occupied laying their eggs or covering over their nests at daybreak. That is when they can be observed under ideal conditions and in a very specific desert environment.

The island of Masirah is also one of the most interesting sites for the observation of sea turtles; however, access is more difficult than at Ra's al Hadd, and there are no tourist facilities, which means that any visit to nesting beaches can take on the quality of a veritable expedition.

This is compensated for by the impression that you are at one of the ends of the earth, far away from your usual trials and tribulations.

PRACTICAL INFORMATION

The best egg laying months are April through August.

TRANSPORTATION

■ **BY PLANE.** Muscat can be reached daily from New York and Washington, DC, via Saudi Arabia Airlines.

■ **BY CAR.** Leaving Muscat, the coastal road is paved for approximately 30 miles (50 km), then it becomes a rocky road. After the town of Sur, the last large village, the road winds almost continuously along the wild coast and passes close to Ra's al Hadd. The only practical option is to have your own vehicle and to travel independently. There are regular bus links between Muscat and Sur—164 feet (50 m) apart, but beyond this locality, the continuation of the trip becomes risky.

A four-wheel drive vehicle can be easily rented in Muscat but this option is very expensive, particularly since an Omani chauffeur must drive it, and it requires a great deal of caution given the difficulties of orientation and identification on the small Omani roads.

ACCOMMODATIONS

Total autonomy is required as there are no restaurants and no place to purchase basic necessities such as food and fuel in the area of the reserve. Drinkable water is also rare.

The town of Sur has several satisfactory establishments, although relatively expensive; in the reserve the only option is camping but visitors must provide their own equipment. Camping is not authorized on the beach or its vicinity so as not to disturb the turtles coming to lay their eggs.

CLIMATE

The main season for green sea turtle reproduction in Ra's al Hadd is our summer, but this season is also the hottest in the north and east of Oman. Days can be truly torrid—up to 113°F and even 122°F (45° to 50°C)! They are thus unbearable for some people. The temperature goes down very little during the night, although the sea breeze occasionally makes the atmosphere somewhat more bearable.

The best time for tourists in Oman is our winter (December to February) when temperatures are very agreeable during the day, although the nights can be cold. Since turtles lay their eggs more or less year-round, it is often possible to observe turtles, especially green sea turtles, in the process of laying their eggs outside of the high season for nesting.

The dominant winds generally blow from the north during this time of year, bringing often violent rains, but primarily affecting the northern slope of the mountains, thus saving the Ra's al Hadd area.

TRAVEL CONDITIONS

An inexpensive visitor's permit is required. Contact the Omani tourist services in Muscat, or in hotels or travel agencies, in order to find out the latest conditions in effect. The situation changes very quickly in Oman with regard to foreign visitors, and it is entirely possible that at the time you are reading this, it will be possible to obtain a visitor's permit directly at the entrance to the reserve.

All-night visits to the beaches must be accompanied by a guide from the reserve. At present, foreigners who make the effort to visit Ra's al Hadd are rare—which can also be noted in the hospitality of the reserve's guards.

The Black Sea Turtle

(*Chelonia agassizii*)
FRENCH: tortue franche du Pacifique

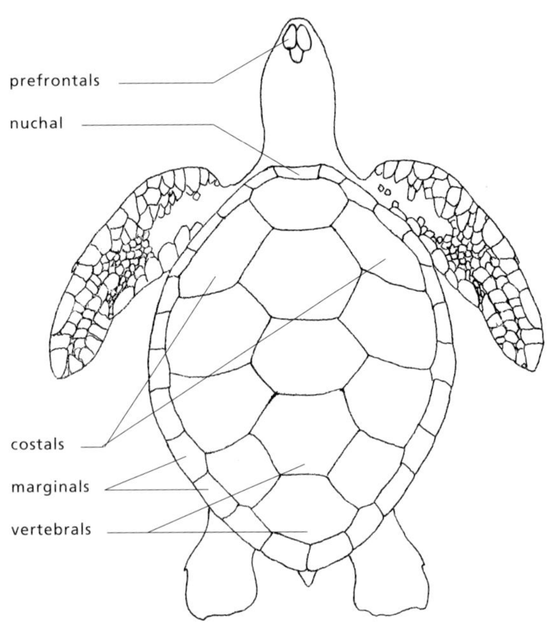

Drawing of the differentiation of *Chelonia agassizii:*
- Identical to *Chelonia mydas,* but blacker on the integument.
- Nuchal does not touch the two first costals.
- Single pair of prefrontals.
- Rounded muzzle.

Description

Measurements: adult 26 to 46 inches (65 to 117 cm). **Average weight:** 330 pounds (150 kg).

This turtle is differentiated from the green sea turtle by its general coloring, which is darker, sometimes almost black, with fine light lines between the plates. Streaks of brown or light olive green are discernable in the young; some older animals have a covering of algae on their **backs** giving them a bright green look. The carapace in adults is often vaulted, with a higher back than in *Chelonia mydas,* especially in large females. There are five vertebral plates, four pairs of laterals, and eleven pairs of marginals.

The **head** is smaller and more uniformly dark, brown, dark green, or black, without the yellow markings seen in the green sea turtle. There is one pair of prefrontals and four postorbitals on each side. The eye is smaller than that of *C. mydas.* The jaws have the same cutting and shearing edges as the green turtle, for grazing on sea grasses. The **flippers** have a single visible claw.

Distribution

Not too long ago, this turtle was considered a subspecies of *C. mydas,* but today it is considered a separate species. The deeply notched shell above the hind limbs and the coloration are two of the major characteristics. It is nonetheless very similar to the green sea turtle, and is sometimes known as the "Pacific green turtle," which indicates its distribution. It is found along the length of the Pacific coast of both North and South America, from Canada as far as Tierra del Fuego, and in the east as far as the Galapagos, where researchers have observed *Chelonia agassizii* that are more colorful and brighter than elsewhere. It is almost never seen in deep ocean waters and prefers the coast; its area of distribution in the Pacific never goes beyond 311 miles (500 km) from the shore. It seems to migrate very little, and the populations of the Galapagos complete their entire life cycle in the area of this archipelago, with the exception of several that have been found in Costa Rica or Peru. Maximum distances of 2,175 miles (3,500 km) have been noted, which is small for a sea turtle. The major nesting beaches are Michoacan in Mexico, Jiquilisco in El Salvador, Quinta Playa in the Galapagos, and Paracas in Peru.

Diet

Algae, which makes up 90 percent of its diet, and aquatic vegetation, as well as sponges, jellyfish, several kinds of fish, and sometimes crustaceans and echinoderms.

Mating

These turtles seem rather particular; observers noted in 1976 that a male-female couple could be consistently followed by a dozen males, each trying to mate with the female or to join the couple. Recent aerial surveillance has shown far fewer males in mating areas (1.04 per couple). Mating is visible at dawn, not far from the nesting beaches.

The male uses the claws on his front flippers and his strong tail to cling to the female's back, creating a strong three-point hold.

Egg Laying

The egg-laying period depends on the latitude. In Mexico, it extends from August to January, peaking in October–November; in the Galapagos, it is from December to June. On the beaches where the olive Ridley sea turtle and the leatherback sea turtle also lay their eggs, the *C. agassizii* lays its eggs between these two species. The same places are used by these three animals, which causes disturbances and destruction between the species. There are approximately three clutches per year, sometimes eight, and the turtle may lay eggs only every two or three years. About 70 eggs are laid, with a maximum of 139 eggs. They are approximately 1.6 inches (42 mm) in size, for a weight of approximately 1.4 ounces (40 g); the incubation period varies between 50 and 55 days. The eggs are eaten by gulls, boars, ghost crabs, pigs, ants, and a type of burrowing beetle, in the Galapagos, but especially the dogs and pigs near villages. In Michoacan, Mexico, females have been killed by wild dogs while laying eggs. On the Revilla Gigedo islands, snakes eat the young turtles, and in the sea, numerous carnivorous fish feast on them, as do sharks on the prowl.

Juveniles resemble those of the green sea turtle. Their carapace and their flippers are very dark on top, brown or black bordered with a lighter narrow edge and white underneath. They then acquire a gray or black coloring.

Hatchlings emerge after dark, and immediately seek the relative safety of the sea. Their carapace is keeled, and the upper beak is light. Juveniles are more carnivorous than the adults, but show greater interest in sea grass than eels as they mature.

Protection

Very little is known of the demography and numbers of this species, which has been less studied than the green sea turtle; however, in Mexico a significant decline in the number of egg layings has been noted. In the 1960s juveniles from this species were sold in pet shops in California and even offered to tourists on some Galapagos beaches. In addition, this turtle was confused with the olive Ridley sea turtle and it was fished to supply Mexican factories. Today, the beaches are better protected, but the species is particularly subject to being caught in shrimp nets and shark nets. Poaching has also been noticed, particularly in South American countries. The total number of *C. agassizii* is certainly not in as marked a decline as that of *Lepidochelys kempii*, but the fact that this animal is less monitored and occupies a restricted area along the coast makes its conservation more risky.

Observation Site

Ecuador: Galapagos Islands

The Galapagos Islands are located in the Pacific Ocean, off the coast of Ecuador, to which they belong. The archipelago consists of some ten principal islands, and a number of important smaller islands sprinkled over enormous marine expanses.

A living laboratory of evolution, the Galapagos has long had a worldwide reputation for the remarkable diversity of their wildlife. Today, they are one of the principal world destinations for nature tourism.

For sea turtles, too, the Galapagos archipelago is a special place; after all, Galapagos means "turtle." Six of the eight current species, in fact, frequent its waters and its beaches, with only the Kemp's Ridley sea turtle and the flatback sea turtle not included.

While the Galapagos is not one of the principal nesting areas for the black sea turtle, this species is well represented there, and can be regularly spotted in the water, immediately off the shores of the archipelago. Specialists believe that the black sea turtles living in the Galapagos Islands spend their entire lives there.

A national park for decades, the Galapagos today is still trying to reconcile the interests of its remarkable flora and fauna, the

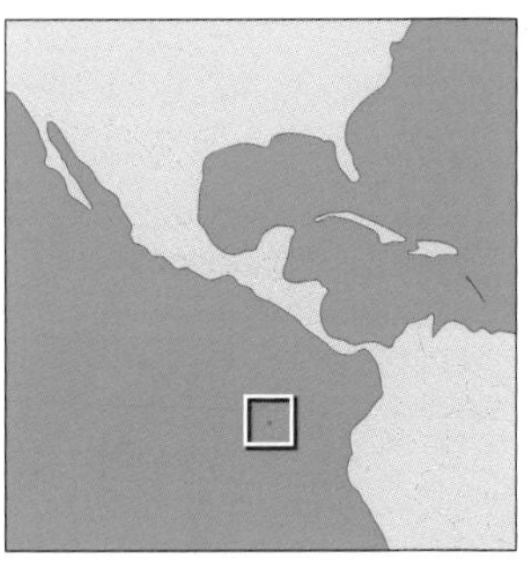

needs of an invasive human population, and the expectations of a very large number of visitors. (The invasive nature of visitors is not new; the islands were known to seafarers as early as the 1600s as a source of wood and fresh tortoise meat.) This constant influx of tourists in an often very fragile natural environment has caused the park administration to considerably restrict access to the islands, now authorized to only 50 tourist sites on the dozen principal islands of the archipelago. All visitors must be accompanied and guided at all times by authorized naturalists.

Fauna and Flora

The dominant natural landscape in the Galapagos Islands is rather arid and rocky. Rocks are interspersed with clumps of dry bushes and shrubs. The pads of the large tree cactus, opuntia, are the only vegetative source of water for the tortoises. The fauna and the flora are particularly noteworthy both for their high level of endemism and their extraordinary familiarity toward man.

Among the best-represented and most spectacular species are the Galapagos penguins, sea lions, various species of land and sea iguanas, and, of course, giant land turtles. The latter are present on many of the principal islands, with each island home to particular subspecies, obvious proof of the phenomenon of evolutionary differentiation still in progress.

Observation

It is not possible to spend the night on the islands, with the exception of several developed areas, so visitors need a great deal of luck to be able to observe sea turtles, particularly black sea turtles, in the process of laying their eggs during the day. On the other hand, during the black sea turtle's peak nesting season, the sometimes remarkable concentration of these turtles can be seen in the sea in immediate proximity to their nesting sites.

Timid and clumsy on land, sea turtles are graceful and facile in the water; just one rip-

The volcanic environment, as superb as it is austere, of the Galapagos Islands.

The Galapagos penguin is one of the most abundant creatures in the spectacular fauna of the archipelago.

ple of a flipper sends the turtle a yard ahead. They generally demonstrate considerable daring in the water; so it is possible to swim close to them without unduly frightening them. The Galapagos Islands are perhaps one of the few places in the world where it is possible to swim with sea turtles, penguins, and sea lions. Two of the principal egg-laying sites are located in the islands of Floreana, also called Santa Cruz, and Santiago.

In Floreana, sea turtles frequent the Punta Corporante Beach, one of the four tourist sites currently open on this island, the others being Asilo de La Paz, Devil's Crown, and Post Office Bay, all three located on the northern coast of the island. The beach is also remarkable for its green hues, caused by the presence of fragments of green-colored crystals. Close by, a small bay known as Flamingo Lagoon often contains groups of pink flamingos and various species of seabirds.

The other egg-laying site for black sea turtles is located off the island of Santiago, on the small islet known as Isla Bartolome. Despite its rather modest size of slightly

Giant Galapagos turtle *(Geochelone elephantopus)*. Each—or almost each—island is home to a specific subspecies of this impressive reptile.

Paradise Condemned?

The Galapagos archipelago was never frequented by Indian tribes; rather, it was the Europeans who discovered, populated, and then devastated these miraculous islands. The profusion of land and sea turtles was for a long time a source of supply for intense commerce with western countries. It was Darwin, in 1835, who made known the large chelonians of the Galapagos, but beginning in 1867 the Republic of Ecuador took possession of the archipelago, and a colony of 200 to 300 individuals banished by the government was established on Charles Island. This so reduced the number of turtles that the colonists sent collectors to other islands (James Island, for example) to capture the turtles in order to salt their meat. These colonists exploited the fauna shamelessly, and harvested sea turtles such as *C. agassizii* on the beaches of Saint Barthélemy where they would come to lay their eggs in large numbers. Today, more than 10,000 peasants and fishermen, sent by the Ecuadoran government to these islands where tourism generates significant revenue, clear the land and the sea of everything that can be exploited: crabs, dolphins, and turtles. On Isabella, land turtles are freely slaughtered "because they disturb growing." This invasion of colonists threatens to decimate the fauna and finally, to keep the tourists away, thus causing both biological and serious economic poverty. Fortunately, after four years of efforts undertaken by the World Conservation Union and scientists, the Ecuadoran government has finally enacted a special law for the preservation of the archipelago. A large budget is devoted to eradicating the goats and donkeys destroying the environment and the program is designed to "significantly reduce human encroachment and mining."

more than 247 acres (100 ha), it is home to large colonies of penguins and is also intensively used by sea turtles during the mating season. Its isolation protects the sea turtles and other animals from the depredations caused by formerly domesticated animals that have been returned to the wild, such as pigs; on the island of Santiago, the pigs destroy up to 85 percent of sea turtle nests in certain places.

PRACTICAL INFORMATION

The high season for black sea turtle nesting is from January to April.

TRANSPORTATION

■ **BY PLANE.** Without a boat, the only way to reach the islands is by plane. There are flights daily only from Quito, the capital of Ecuador, via Guayaquil. The islands are 932 miles (1,500 km) from Ecuador.

■ **BY GUIDED TOUR.** There is no regular link for passengers between the various islands, most of the area of which is included in the national park, and for which access is strictly regulated. It is better to sign up at home or in Ecuador for a guided tour; many tourist agencies offer trips to the Galapagos Islands, particularly in Quito. It is, in fact, very difficult to visit the islands on one's own, and impossible to do so without authorization.

ACCOMMODATIONS

There are few possibilities for accommodations on the islands. Just about all the visitors who stay in the Galapagos for more than one day go there by boat, on which they spend the night.

CLIMATE

The hot and rainy season runs from January to June; the dry, cool season runs from July to December.

The daytime temperatures are generally pleasant but the evenings and the nights can be cool when it is rainy or when there are strong ocean winds.

TRAVEL CONDITIONS

Access to the Galapagos Islands is heavily regulated, with only a limited number of sites open for visitors; therefore, the only realistic option is to participate in an organized tour. All of these measures, which have become necessary due to the increasing number of visitors, have, of course, as their purpose the maximum preservation of the natural integrity of this archipelago that is unique in all the world.

A very real benefit to the traveler, however, is the wide knowledge of natural history possessed by your co-tour members.

The Loggerhead Sea Turtle

(Caretta caretta)
FRENCH: tortue caouanne

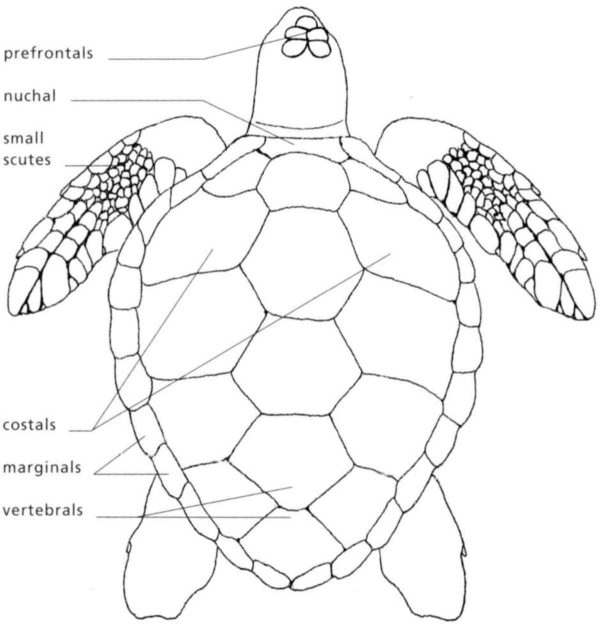

Drawing of the differentiation of *Caretta caretta:*
- Nuchal in contact with the first costals.
- Four or five prefrontals.
- Width reaching two thirds of the length.
- On the forward flippers, there are four rows of small scutes between the large plates.

Description

Measurements: 45 inches (115 cm) maximum.
Average weight: 352 pounds (160 kg) maximum.

The loggerhead turtle is somewhat smaller than the green sea turtle, less elongated than *Chelonia mydas*, and clearly cordiform (heart-shaped). The **back** has five pairs of costals, of which the first touch the nuchale shell, with a central keel that is particularly visible in juveniles; each vertebra forms a slight point, occasionally present in adults and particularly pronounced at the front of the back. There are often 12 to 13 marginal scales on each side, but this number can vary from 11 to 15, which is rare in sea turtles. The edge of the marginals is serrated in juveniles, and flattened out in adults.

The **carapace** ranges from dark brown to yellow-orange, or tending toward chocolate-colored, with the edges of the marginals yellow-orange. The plastron is yellow-orange to brown, smooth in adults and doubly keeled in juveniles, and lighter in the latter. The bridges are marked by three large inframarginal shells.

It has a large **head**, rather round as in the green turtle, brown-orange on top, or gray to brown on the underside of the head, and a yellow-orange neck, with a slightly less pronounced beak that is slightly or not at all serrated, and smaller eyes, four or five prefrontals, and generally three postocular shells. It has slightly prominent nostrils. There are brown or gray flippers on the top, yellowish underneath, well adapted for swimming, powerful, and covered with large scales, each equipped with two claws.

Males have a long, wide tail.

Distribution

This species is the most widely distributed after the green sea turtle, and one of the most exploited by man. Its distribution is worldwide, except in the eastern Pacific, from the Galapagos Islands to the coast of South America, where the *Chelonia agassizii* is found, and it can live in colder waters than *C. mydas* (Canada, Nova Scotia, southern Norway, Russia, Japan). They have even been found in the cold waters at 70 degrees north latitude, near Murmansk, and around Rio de la Plata, in Argentina, at 35.5 degrees south, which proves that it is capable of conserving an internal temperature that is higher than its surroundings. It has also been observed in a lethargic state, inert on the bottom, as in Florida, or floating on the surface, as in the Mediterranean.

The loggerhead is seen along the Mediterranean perimeter, where it is the most abundant sea turtle, and, off the coast of France. In Greece it is seen basking in the sun, often escorted by pilot fish that rid it of the parasites or larvae that adhere to its shell.

Only somewhat pelagic, it likes to stay close to the coastline, which makes it possible to be easily observed when diving, or even from the bridge of a ship. It seems to be migratory.

Diet

Mostly carnivorous—mollusks, crustaceans, small fish, and echinoderms. Until the age of four to five years, it feeds on mollusks and planktonic crustaceans, trying not to ingest carnivorous fish. Adults occasionally consume sea grasses and algae. Many Florida turtles are dying after eating penshell bivalves poisoned by red-tide algae.

Mating

Mating is particularly visible on the surface; the male can easily attach himself to the back of the female thanks to the two claws on his forward flippers. Sexual maturity occurs very early, and can begin at four years of age when the turtle can then reach 24 inches (60 cm).

Egg Laying

Nesting beaches are distributed throughout the subtropical and temperate zones of many oceans. The most frequented are those of the island of Masirah in Oman, and in Florida, but they are also found in northern Australia and on the east coast of Africa. Almost everywhere it uses the same nesting beaches as other species. In the Mediterranean it is seen in Greece, Turkey, and Cyprus, and even occasionally in Israel and Libya. Not too long ago it still nested in Corsica, but for several decades it seems to have left this overurbanized island.

Egg laying takes place in the spring or at the beginning of the summer, according to the hemispheres. Females make long migrations from feeding areas. As

For some crabs, such as the *Planes minutus,* turtles are like the hull of a ship to which they attach themselves in order to travel.

with other species, egg laying takes place at nightfall or during the day, when the tide is rising. Up to seven clutches may be laid during the season, every 12 to 15 days. A single hole, dug from 10 to 20 inches (25 to 50 cm) in depth, receives an average of 100 eggs (160 maximum). These eggs are round, white, with a wrinkled shell and a diameter of between 1.4 and 1.9 inches (35 to 49 mm). For this animal, which is particularly fearful, the act of laying is very rapid, taking less than one hour. If she is disturbed while digging her nest, she can return to the sea without laying her eggs; therefore, observation requires a great deal of prudence and calm. Incubation lasts between 46 and 71 days and the critical temperature must be around 86°F (30°C). Above 89.6°F (32°C) there will be only females, and below 82.4°F (28°C) only males. At 86°F (30°C), 60 percent will be female, which is certainly the average sex ratio for the species. When they are born, juveniles have a brown to gray carapace. Turtles born in Florida and in the Caribbean spend their early years in the floating algae of the Sargasso Sea.

Protection

This species is highly endangered, as its nesting sites are often disturbed by urbanization and tourism and it suffers from the pollution of the ocean. In addition, it was heavily hunted over the centuries for its flesh and its carapace. Not too long ago, in the French Antilles, the heads of loggerhead sea turtles impaled on pieces of wood were still being sold.

Drift nets are dangerous for them, as are shrimp nets; the migratory habits of this species increase the dangers to which it is exposed. The use of the TED device carried at the bottom of nets, which makes it possible to save about 60 percent of the turtles caught by shrimp nets, is now obligatory in portions of the Mediterranean, and in 1998 the European Union signed a treaty prohibiting the use of drift nets, which goes into effect in 2002.

The loggerhead sea turtle arrives on Mediterranean shores at the end of spring then departs in September. Adults are rarely seen; for the most part these are subadults 12 to 16 inches (30 to 40 cm) long. In order to better understand the relationship between these Mediterranean turtles and those of the Atlantic, DNA markers were used. It appears that the populations are rather isolated from each other, despite the migratory tendency of this species; therefore, there is good reason to protect the Mediterranean loggerheads, as it is not certain that their populations can be reinforced with individuals from the Atlantic. In Zakynthos, Greece, where the loggerhead sea turtle is the "star" animal, volunteers of a very dynamic organization monitor the nesting beaches day and night, during the entire loggerhead incubation period. Beaches have been acquired by the World Wildlife Fund (WWF) in order to preserve their management, and to avoid the construction of tourist complexes.

On Zakynthos, in Greece, tourism is invading the beaches and causing the remaining turtles that come there to lay their eggs to flee.

Still on Zakynthos, hatcheries are monitored by eco-volunteers, but swimmers are never far away.

Observation Site

U.S. (Florida): Cape Canaveral National Coastal Reserve

Both coasts of Florida are nesting sites for sea turtles. On the southwest coast, loggerheads regularly nest on Sanibel Island. Their nest sites are monitored and protected by Caretta Research, Inc. The southeast coast of the United States constitutes one of the principal nesting areas for loggerhead sea turtles. Florida alone has many nesting beaches that are important for this species, and specifically at the Cape Canaveral National Coastal Reserve, located along Florida's Atlantic Coast, approximately 62 miles (100 km) east of Orlando.

Cape Canaveral, of course, became famous for being home to the principal site for the launching of NASA space rockets, the Kennedy Space Center. Although the enormous installations on the base have had, and continue to have, an impact on the natural environment, they seem not to have had a serious effect on the presence and the nesting of loggerhead sea turtles in the vicinity. The Space Center, in fact, occupies only a rather small portion of Cape Canaveral, a wide peninsula projecting into the Atlantic Ocean. Except for the NASA installations, the entire region has been only slightly affected by development and urbanization, and a significant portion of the area of the Cape is occupied by protected natural sites.

The reserve includes approximately 25 miles (40 km) of protected coast; this is a sandy beach, rather wild, and often swept by winds and ocean waves, behind which large sections of forest extend, for the most part marshy. The Florida pine dominates.

The reserve is frequented by surfers and is highly regarded by the residents of Orlando. The central section, known as Klondike Beach, remains the most interesting from the naturalist point of view and is also the least visited part of the reserve.

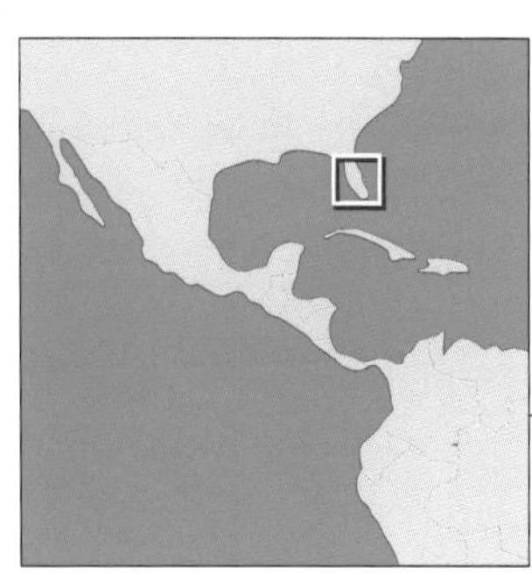

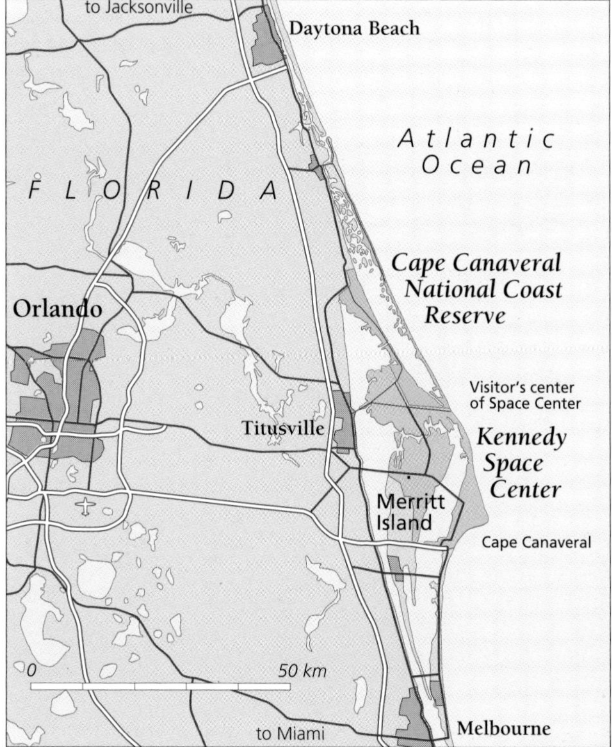

South of Cape Canaveral National Coastal Reserve there is another large animal reserve, the Merritt Island National Wildlife Refuge, which is mainly characterized by brackish, swampy areas, the same as the Cape Canaveral National Coastal Reserve, but without the coast.

Reptiles are often the victims of other reptiles.

Fauna and Flora

The Cape Canaveral reserve is home to numerous, diversified fauna. The avifauna is particularly abundant there; it is easy to observe marine and coastal species, freshwater species typical of swampy environments, or even species belonging to more wooded environments. In the spring and fall, the local

Egrets are among the most common waders in Florida.

Indians and Turtles

The Indians of Florida venerated turtles, and many of their myths are connected with these animals; for instance, one says that in the beginning, there was nothing but a vast ocean and it was on the back of a sea turtle that the first woman had to sit to shape the earth and man out of clay. The Indians ate freshwater turtles, *Malaclemys terrapin,* called the diamondback terrapin, which was widely used as a basic food, and *Trachemys scripta* or yellowbelly slider. There is no information on the use of sea turtles, these chelonians having been particularly exploited by the white man from the beginning of the nineteenth century. A vast warehouse in Key West, at the tip of Florida, was constructed to house thousands of turtles in natural pools, before they were shipped to major cities to be made into turtle soup, steaks, or tortoiseshell for craftsmen.

Two products still harvested in large quantities in Key West 50 years ago (seen here, at the turn of the twentieth century): turtles and sponges.

population is increased by the presence of large groups of migratory birds, primarily seabirds. The reserve, in fact, is a migratory stop for large numbers of birds during the long voyage that leads them along the length of the Atlantic to their warmer winter habitats, or takes them back to their northern nesting areas.

In the forest and on the edge of the swampland, it is sometimes possible to observe mammals such as the Virginia deer and the wild pig. The raccoon, omnipresent, can also easily be seen. The timid manatee spends part of the year in the reserve, sharing the aquatic environment with alligators, which are numerous and occasionally impressive, but generally harmless.

The reserve is also home to several species of carnivorous freshwater turtles, some of which are capable of reaching respectable size, such as the snapping turtle.

Observation

The loggerhead sea turtle—3,000 to 4,000 females per year, on average—is the most numerous. Along with the leatherback sea turtle, it comes to lay eggs on the beaches of the Cape Canaveral National Coastal Reserve. The laying of eggs by loggerhead sea turtles occurs sporadically throughout the year at Cape Canaveral, but the principal nesting season takes place between May and August, with hatching occurring from July to October.

From May to August, it is possible to view them in the reserve. In groups of 20 people, maximum, visitors can visit the beach at the end of the evening and observe, under the guidance of rangers or volunteers, the various phases of the turtle's work.

In Florida, sea turtles were not exploited as intensely as in other Central and South American countries, but the total population of this species has declined considerably as a result of habitat modification, accidental capture in fishing nets, as well as the proliferation of raccoons. In the early 1980s, in fact, raccoons were responsible for destroying up to 95 percent of the loggerhead nests. An important program of conservation was undertaken in 1984, in which the majority of turtle nests in the reserve today are systematically protected by grills, which makes predation by raccoons impossible. This project requires a large number of personnel such as reserve guards and volunteers to patrol the nesting beaches at night during the main nesting period. Females are banded, and various measures are conducted for scientific purposes. These conservation activities have made it possible to reduce the predation of nests by at least 15 percent, and the total number of loggerhead sea turtles has progressively increased in the area. The problem of fire ant nest invasion has not yet been solved, and indeed it is generally only detected after a nest has failed to hatch and is opened for investigation.

The raccoon is a formidable plunderer of sea turtle nests in Cape Canaveral, Florida.

PRACTICAL INFORMATION

May to August are the best months to observe egg laying, July to October for hatching.

TRANSPORTATION

■ **BY PLANE.** Visitors arrive via the Orlando airport, which is one of the largest and busiest in the southeastern United States.

■ **BY CAR.** It is possible to rent a car in Orlando relatively inexpensively. From Orlando. travel toward the east, in the direction of the Kennedy Space Center. When you reach the Space Center's visitor's center, travel north for a good 6 miles (10 km) before reaching the reserve.

■ **BY BUS.** Connections by bus also leave Orlando for the coast and the Kennedy Space Center.

DISTANCES

Orlando—Kennedy Space Center: approximately 58 miles (90 km).

Kennedy Space Center—Cape Canaveral National Coastal Reserve: 6 miles (10 km).

ACCOMMODATIONS

It is possible to camp inside the reserve, specifically on the beach, but only on official campsites, which are free and well equipped with running water, electricity, and toilets. They can be busy during school vacation periods.

CLIMATE

The climate is generally warm in the summer, while significant differences may be noted between May and July and August. Average day time temperatures are generally around 77°F (25°C), and the air is very humid. The sea breeze can cool down the temperature, and the evenings become cool. It can rain at any time, but most of the annual rainfall, primarily tropical in nature, occurs during the summer.

TRAVEL CONDITIONS

The Cape Canaveral National Coastal Reserve is administered by the National Parks Service.

Nocturnal visits to the beach to observe turtles laying their eggs are well organized and regulated; each visitor is made part of a group, and guided by a ranger or an officially authorized volunteer. They are very familiar with sea turtles, and can therefore provide very interesting information. Visits are free.

In peak periods, you must reserve the visit by calling (1)-407-267-1110.

The reserve needs volunteers to participate in the monitoring of egg laying and in guiding visitors. For information, call the above telephone number.

Observation Site

Brazil (Espirito Santo): Guriri

Brazil occupies a key position for sea turtles in South America. Four species of turtles frequent its waters and use its beaches at various degrees for the laying of eggs: the green sea turtle, the olive Ridley, the hawksbill, and the leatherback. A fifth species, the loggerhead, is classified as a "possible" visitor by the CCC. Of the approximately 4,661 miles (7,500 km) of the country's coast, only the stretch between Rio de Janeiro and the border with French Guiana is used by sea turtles for nesting; this represents almost 3,728 miles (6,000 km). The five species lay their eggs on continental beaches, with the exception of the green sea turtle, which prefers ocean islands, such as the Fernando de Noronha archipelago or the island of Trinidad.

In the early 1980s the decline and extinction of all of the species of sea turtles seemed inevitable, as these animals were the victims of generalized persecution on the part of coastal inhabitants—massacres of adult turtles, systematic pillage of nests for the consumption and commercialization of eggs, capture at sea, and so on. It is considered

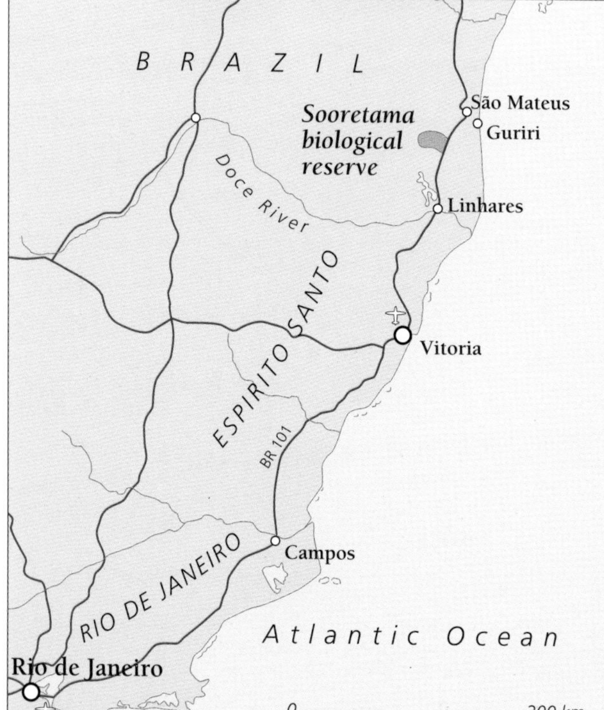

that in a period of only 20 years, almost one half of the population of sea turtles was destroyed in Brazil.

In 1980 an ambitious project for the protection of these animals was begun along the entire length of the coast: project PRO TAMAR (TArtarugas MARinas). This project is ongoing and the results obtained by IBAMA, the government administration responsible for the protection of nature, and the various associations involved in the protection of turtles are truly remarkable. This project, often cited as an example, has made it possible to reduce poaching to almost nothing on the beaches actively monitored by the project, and to reduce it primarily through the absence of commercial outlets for turtle meat and eggs.

One of the priority strategies of the promoters of the project was to substantially involve the coastal population in the protection of sea turtles; a significant portion of these efforts is devoted to programs for educating the population.

Today, PRO TAMAR monitors almost 621 miles (1,000 km) of the coast of Brazil. In season it employs several hundred employees who come, for the most part, from the villages near the coast. Former poachers were the first to be employed by the project, which directly benefited from the experience of these former destroyers of turtles. Someone who has grown up living with (and dependent upon) sea turtles knows a lot about these animals. In return, these individuals receive, a steady income that enables them to feed their families, and serve as respected emissaries for PRO TAMAR.

Fourteen stations for the artificial incubation of eggs are distributed along the coast; since the beginning of the project, two and a half million young turtles have been incubated and protected. Eggs laid in the immediate proximity of a village, and thus endangered by human activities, are systematically removed after being laid, and placed in an incubation unit.

Recently, PRO TAMAR expanded its activities to include the protection of feeding sites for the turtles located off the coast, specifically by studying fishing methods that respect the animals as well as the marine environment in general.

Three incubation stations are distributed along the coast of the Brazilian state of Espirito Santo, north of the state of Rio de Janeiro, approximately 149 miles (240 km) north of Vitoria, the capital of Espirito Santo. The

Today, thanks to the efforts of project PRO TAMAR, sea turtle nests are opened only by scientists.

Guriri station is one of these and includes research and monitoring units, an incubation unit, and a visitor's center.

The station administers more than 25 miles (40 km) of protected beaches for sea turtles; four of the five species of sea turtles present in Brazil come to lay their eggs in this region. Only a few human installations, in general close to Guriri, are distributed along this part of the coast, which thus remains rather wild.

Fauna and Flora

Sea turtles are among the most remarkable animals here.

The protected zone has many huge sand dunes, and is home to several beautiful areas of mangroves. Avifauna is rich and varied. Mammals however, are less remarkable, the destruction of coastal forests, formerly inside the territory, having caused the natural cover to disappear over large areas. Along with the disappearance of the smaller mammals, the larger predators, such as jaguarundis and other cats, are gone.

In the Sooretama biological reserve, some 19 miles (30 km) southeast of Guriri, it is possible to see several species of primates—tamarins, among others—all more or less endangered throughout their area of distribution in the Atlantic regions of Brazil.

Observation

It is possible to observe sea turtles laying their eggs on the beaches of Guriri during the peak season, which corresponds to our winter. There is no infrastructure for visitors, but it is possible to obtain information about turtles from the village or from the project PRO TAMAR station. Diplomacy and prudence should be used, since the station is not a tourist center.

We recommend that visitors use caution during their nocturnal visits to the beach, in order not to disturb either the activities of the sea turtles, or those of the members of project PRO TAMAR.

The very specific environment of the mangrove.

Villagers Save Turtles

In general, coastal villages are not much concerned with the protection of turtles, and even live by exploiting them. In Brazil, this situation has resulted in a significant decline in certain species, such as the olive Ridley (*xbirro* in Brazilian), or the hawksbill (*tartaruga de pente*). Fortunately, since the establishment of PRO TAMAR, protection stations, managed by villagers and thus providing revenue to former fishermen, are preventing the destruction of local fauna. In Regencia, for example, 5 miles (8 km) from Comboios, all of the villagers engage in "turtle culture"—women create crafts for the foundation, and the village has opened a hotel, as well as a museum and a library devoted to turtles. This has made it possible for the villagers to survive without killing turtles or collecting eggs. According to the director of the Comboios station, much still remains to be done so that this new vision of preservation becomes instilled in the minds of the villagers, but it is surely by this common work between protectors and local populations that Brazilian fauna will be preserved.

Children are always appreciative of young sea turtles, but it is better not to handle these juveniles, which must return to the sea as quickly as possible.

PRACTICAL INFORMATION

Guriri is a small seaside resort frequented principally by Brazilians, and where western tourists are rare.

TRANSPORTATION

BY PLANE. Regular flights are provided to Rio de Janeiro by Varig and Avianca from New York, Miami, and Los Angeles. American Airlines flies from Miami as well. The route that follows the coast toward the north leads to Vitoria.

BY BUS. The BR-101 national road connects the city of Linhares, north of Vitoria, to that of Sao Mateus. There are regular bus connections from the regional capital to Sao Mateus. It is also possible to rent a car in Vitoria, but it is more expensive.

BY TAXI. Connections between Sao Mateus and Guriri are somewhat haphazard. At best, visitors without their own cars can make the trip by taxi, arranging with the driver for the return voyage.

DISTANCES

Rio de Janeiro—Vitoria: 342 miles (550 km)

Vitoria—Guriri: 149 miles (240 km)

Linhares—Sao Mateus: 75 miles (120 km)

Sao Mateus—Guriri: 7 miles (12 km)

ACCOMMODATIONS

Lodging in Guriri is generally not up to our standards; however, there are more possibilities for lodging in Sao Mateus with variable levels of comfort.

CLIMATE

The reproductive season for sea turtles corresponds more or less with our winter (October to February), which is the humid season along the Brazilian coast. Precipitation is abundant, and the air is often saturated with humidity.

Average daytime temperatures are generally between 77° and 86°F (25° and 30°C), and there is little fluctuation between day and night. The sea breezes fortunately make the atmosphere more pleasant.

TRAVEL CONDITIONS

Access to the Guriri is not subject to any specific regulation.

The Hawksbill Sea Turtle

(*Eretmochelys imbricata*)
FRENCH: tortue imbriqué, tortue caret

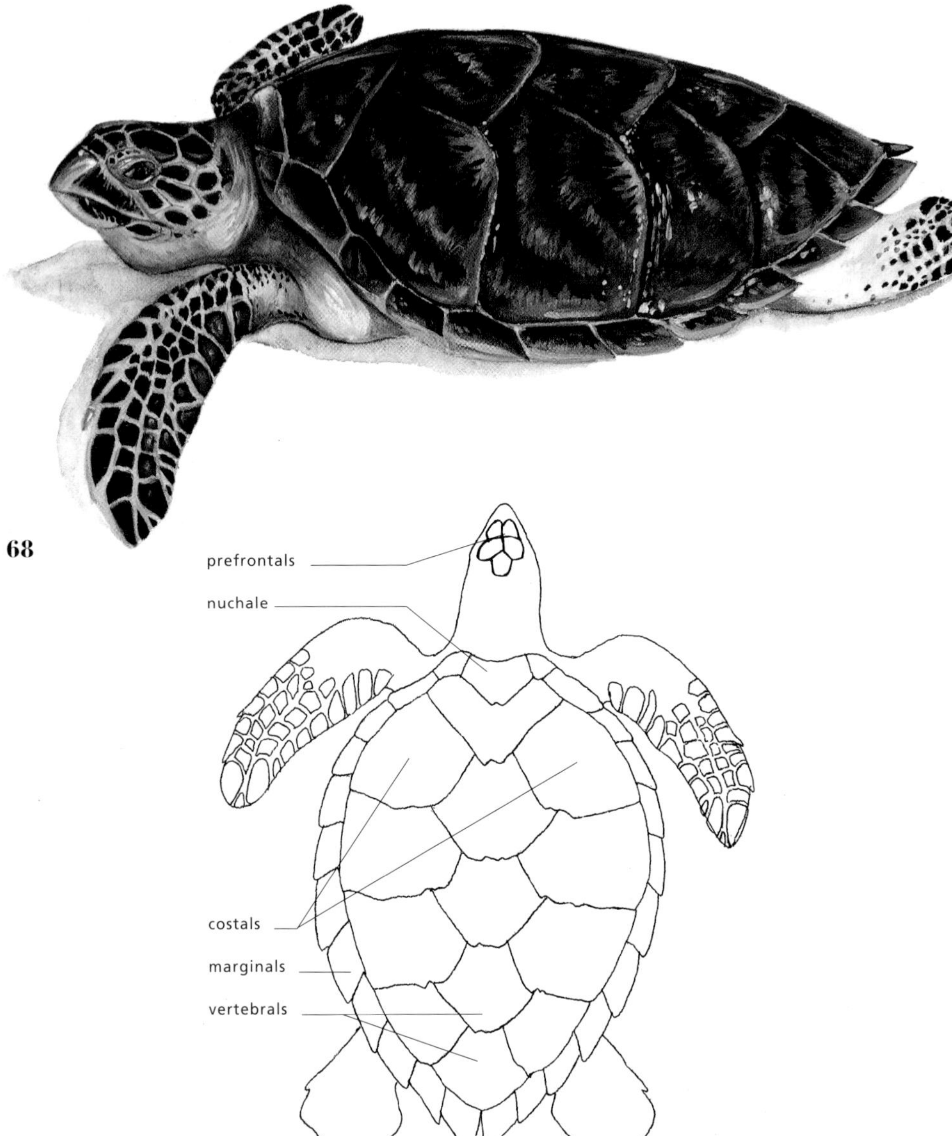

Drawing of the differentiation of *Eretmochelys imbricata:*
- Nuchal does not touch the first costals.
- Two pairs of prefrontals.
- Elongated muzzle.
- Scutes on the back overlap like tiles on a roof.

Description

Measurements: 37 inches (95 cm) maximum
Average weight: 132 pounds (60 kg); record: 306 pounds (139 kg)

This is the most elongated of the seven sea turtles with a hard carapace.

The **carapace** is brown-red to beige-orange, with dark brown marbling, black, or cream or yellow streaks, clearly cordiform with a rather marked posterior point; remarkable by the overlapping of its shells, each superimposed on the other. There are four pairs of costals, with the first not touching the nuchale shell. Lateral marginals are very narrow with larger posteriors forming significant serrations, especially in the young. Contrasting spots and colorations disappear with age, and when the turtle reaches 24 inches (60 cm), the beauty of its back declines; with time it becomes smooth.

The **plastron** is yellowish white, sometimes dark (brown-orange), streaked, or marked with spots of cream, rather wide, and doubly serrated. Serration is more pronounced in juveniles. Its powerful **flippers** are rather delicate and covered with large dark scales on the top, underlined with light lines. There are two claws on each. The skin and underside of the flippers and tail are yellow, darker at the extremities.

The **head** is narrow and rather small, the beak is rather hooked, recalling a raptor—hence its name. On the top are two pairs of prefrontal shells and a frontal in the form of a shield. The head is red to brown on the top, with narrow yellow lines; yellow dominates on the sides; brown spots become blurred.

Two subspecies can be distinguished: that of the Atlantic Ocean *(E. imbricata imbricata)* and that of the Pacific and Indian Oceans *(E. i. bissa)*. The latter is wider and more cordiform, with more pronounced serration. The flippers and head are darker in color.

Distribution

There is a wide distribution area over most tropical areas of the world and specifically the Indian Ocean. This turtle

In the area of Aldabra, north of Madagascar, the waters recede, revealing a superb sea turtle that has come to this quiet island to feed.

is a denizen of rocky coastlines and coral reefs. It nests on numerous tropical and subtropical beaches, especially in the Caribbean, the Red Sea, the Mascarenes, northern Australia, Indonesia, and Malaysia. It formerly nested in French Guiana and still returns to Martinique and Guadalupe. Some individuals have been seen in the Mediterranean near Albania and the French coast, but these observations are rare, and they do not nest there.

Diet

This is the most omnivorous of turtles. When young, it is almost herbivorous, then it becomes interested in octopus and invertebrates, in crabs, and in coral, which it gnaws with its beak; it can often be seen under the water engaged in this gnawing behavior.

Mating

Its reproductive age is unknown. Mating takes place close to nesting beaches, in shallow waters. Copulation can take several hours, and the males are so forward they pursue the females right up to the beach. It is unknown if mating occurs at any other time or place.

Egg Laying

For laying eggs, the hawksbill turtle prefers isolated areas, where lush vegetation makes it possible to hide. Its nest consists of a single hole, rather deep—up to 24 inches (60 cm). Egg laying takes place at night at high tide, but the species does not seem afraid of light, which makes it possible for observers to take good pictures. The duration of egg laying and the manner of digging are similar to that of *Chelonia mydas*. There may be three or four clutches laid during the season, spaced 15 days apart, sometimes 2 or 3 days, sometimes 45 days. There are a great number of eggs—from 50 to 200—which is explained by their rather small size—between 1.4 and 1.7 inches (35 and 44 mm). These eggs are spherical and white, with a wrinkled membrane. The incubation period lasts from 58 to 75 days. The hatchlings have a brown-red carapace, with lighter marginals, a vertebral keel, and serrations on

Hawksbill sea turtles were widely used in poor countries to make tourist items. With the total protection of sea turtles, only the use of existing stock is still authorized, but their transport is prohibited. Artists must resort to using other raw materials.

the back marginals. Their average weight is 0.5 ounce (15 g). Ghost crabs are very fond of them, as are dogs and wild pigs.

The newborn has a reddish brown carapace, with lighter marginals, a vertebral keel, and serrations on the back marginals. Its average weight is about 0.5 ounce (15 g).

Conservation

It is a sad fact that the beautiful shells on the back of this species have caused it to be hunted by man more than are other species. Also considered the most beautiful of sea turtles, it often ends up as a trophy. It was formerly distributed throughout the temperate waters of the world, but this is no longer the case.

In the sixteenth century, in Europe, young hawksbill turtles were bred where there was no sunlight and with a very rich diet, so that they would grow quickly but their shell would remain blond and light. In Asia they were boiled alive so their shells would become detached, and they were then released into the sea, in hopes that their shells would regenerate. Three centuries ago, there existed famous furniture that was covered with this much sought-after product. In the 1940s and 1950s a luxury trade developed in France, based on tortoiseshell, for the manufacture of all types of objects. Today, around the world, people continue to buy jewels, boxes, or combs made of tortoiseshell. In Japan, between 1970 and 1990, more than 1 million pounds (710,000 kg) of tortoiseshell were imported! While this species is now protected, stocks of tortoiseshell were built up, which will make it possible for artisans to work on this material for many years to come; in addition, traffic continues in many countries, as does illegal culling. In Bali, despite the boycott begun by Greenpeace in the 1980s, the killing of 30 turtles (green or hawksbill) is authorized every week for sacrifices. Opposite Benoa, on the southern point of the island, a group of women is devoted to hauling turtles. This spectacle is distressing. The turtles are attached by the fore flippers with a solid iron wire, then two or three animals are hung on bamboo perches, carried by two women, who then put them into floating cages filled with brackish water. There, without care or food, the animals wait several weeks for the day of the sacrifice.

This species is still hunted for its flesh in the Caribbean, in New Guinea, and in the Solomon Islands; in Indonesia the eggs are consumed. But the most disturbing is the destruction of nesting beaches, as in Sri Lanka, Malaysia, or the Caribbean.

Artificial enclosures have been put into place in some countries such as Samoa, Mexico, and Malaysia, but it is the interest in tortoiseshell that decorators and elegant society members must be made to forget. In Japan, in recent years, an artificial tortoiseshell has been developed that may replace the real one, and will hopefully save many turtles.

Observation Site

Sri Lanka: Bentota Beach

The majority of sandy beaches and bays that fill this island are frequented, in various degrees, by sea turtles. One of the most intensely visited areas is the southwest coast of the island, specifically the part located south of the capital, Colombo. The hawksbill turtle reproduces in significant numbers in Sri Lanka; other species such as the green sea turtle, which is the most frequent, the loggerhead, and the olive Ridley are, however, less numerous.

Sea turtles have suffered and continue to suffer a great deal because of man in Sri Lanka, especially in the country's northwest portion. All laws aside, it is unrealistic to ask a man or a woman not to take a sea turtle when there are hungry family members at home. Thus, despite legal protection measures on their behalf, they are still hunted for their flesh, their eggs are highly valued, and therefore their nests are more or less systematically pillaged. Numerous turtles perish following the intensification of fishing practices, and many beaches have been lost to turtles following urbanization for the purposes of tourism. Nevertheless, very valuable efforts have occasionally been undertaken in various locations throughout the island in order to provide sea turtles with the best chance for survival in the future. One of the most interesting projects, and perhaps one of the most attractive, is one that has been pursued for several years in the area of Bentota, south of Colombo, by a local team of villagers directed by the tireless Kitshiri. This young man, specifically motivated to save turtles, is conducting an admirable battle despite obstacles that are considered almost insurmountable. The Turtle Research Project, located in South Bentota, has a protected incubation area that can be visited by tourists. Since the beginning of the project, initiated and managed entirely by young villagers, this enclosure, guarded day and night, has made it possible to save tens of thousands of young turtles, a remarkable result when one knows that a single egg, sold in city shops, represents approximately the daily salary of a waiter in a seaside hotel. To protect these eggs, they are purchased from the villagers and placed under monitored incubation. The educational aspect of the project is also very important; the schoolchildren of Bentota and neighboring villages come regularly to visit the enclosure to learn about the animals.

Recently, a project national in scope was begun by the Sri Lankan authorities for the purpose of better protecting the nesting

areas of sea turtles, specifically on the nearby coast of Bentota. It is hoped that this project may quickly reverse the current trend, as time is growing short for the sea turtles of this island to be protected.

Fauna and Flora

Sri Lanka has been world famous for many years for the diversity of its fauna and flora; in a relatively reduced area, this tropical island, in fact, has many varied natural environments that differ greatly from each other.

In the north and east of Sri Lanka are the last of the island's great forest areas to have escaped deforestation. The forest is dry and deciduous; it is also possible to

Tea plantations have replaced forest over thousands of acres in Sri Lanka.

The urbanized and heavily frequented beaches are, in Sri Lanka as elsewhere, slowly being deserted by sea turtles.

find areas of dry savannah interspersed with farms. To the west and south is the area subject to monsoons, converted primarily into plantations and farms. In the center, the high mountains, which reach 8,279 feet (2,524 m), still contain some large pockets of high-altitude humid forest between tea plantations. Finally, in the south there are still some important areas of mangroves. Sri Lankan avifauna is rich, and hundreds of species can be found there. Where there are lots of birds, predator birds tend to be found as well. Nocturnal visitors may be amused to sight the barn owl, *Tyto alba*, the same type of bird commonly found in our North American woodlands, seeking rodent prey. The large fauna contains the majority of species that can be found on the Indian subcontinent: chital and sambar deer, water buffaloes, boars, leopards, primates, and others. The tiger is the most notable animal not found among the large Singhalese fauna. Elephants, threatened by ever-increasing human pressure, are the subject of major efforts by the authorities to assure their protection.

Sri Lanka has close to 25 important national parks and reserves, as well as a large number of smaller sanctuaries, which cover almost 13 percent of the total area of the country, a record in the region. The insecurity caused by the rebellion of the Tamil community, which has affected the northern part, and in a lesser way the east of Sri Lanka, for decades makes a certain number of these protected sites inaccessible to foreign visitors, and it is unlikely that this situation will improve in the near future.

The fauna that can be observed in the area of Bentota is not very rich or diversified, this region having been subject to the influence of man. Omnipresent birds are perhaps the principal land attraction in this portion of the coast, whose true natural riches are found beneath the water, where the extraordinary diversity of the coral environment can be discovered.

Observation

Hawksbill turtles can be seen more or less throughout the year on the beaches of the Bentota area, but the best period for observing them is from December to February, for

The Example of Dr. Chandrarisi

In the East, few examples for the protection of nature are as promising as the work of Dr. Chandrarisi. Although turtles have always been exploited in Sri Lanka, a center for the safeguarding of sea turtles was constructed in 1979, in Koskoda, 37 miles (60 km) south of Colombo. A well-known camera manufacturer, Victor Hasselblad, had the idea for this center, and financed it. Dr. Chandrarisi became the director and the organizer, and it is on him alone that the future of this center depends. The idea is to collect eggs that have been illegally collected by the villagers, and place them in enclosures in order to make large releases into the ocean possible. These eggs sold for several rupees apiece, bringing economic well-being to the local populations, and their placement in enclosures avoids the extinction of the species. The Koskoda center is located on the edge of the beach, and consists of several wood buildings, some pools for the young turtles, and natural enclosures in the dunes. The eggs are placed in the incubator, and 70 days after their emergence, the newborns are released into the Indian Ocean. In order to limit attacks by weasels, mongooses, or raptors, mesh covers are installed. The hatching rate is 90 percent, which is very satisfying. This center is in strong contrast with what is taking place in the northern part of the island, where turtles are still collected and massacred. The example of Koskoda and this ecotourism success may influence other villages, thus preserving sea turtles. The only problem is lack of funds. Dr. Chandrarisi is worried, as he receives aid only from tourists, which is hardly enough for the center to function. Some 30,000 turtles were freed into the ocean last year, but he would like to do more. It is up to us, the visitors, to help him.

The hatcheries of Sri Lanka, well monitored, produce many juveniles, which will serve to recreate natural populations.

the laying of eggs, and from February to April, for hatching. Since this is the case in almost every location where hawksbill turtles lay their eggs, there are no spectacular concentrations of this retiring species, which, in addition, has the peculiarity of having to dig its nest in areas of heavy vegetation, where it can go unremarked. The young emerge from the nests late at night or in early morning. By some method they hatch almost simultaneously, and all scramble to the surface.

All along the coast, villagers are happy—for a fee, of course—to guide visitors to see the turtles when they come to lay their eggs. Often, such activities take place in a rather anarchic, disorderly fashion, which is as much of a pity for the villagers as for the turtles. Well-managed tourism for observing turtles may, in fact, constitute a considerable economic resource for the local village populations and may also contribute to the protection of sea turtles.

The Turtle Research Project of Bentota is perhaps the exception. The members of the project can assist visitors with the observation of turtles that have come to lay their eggs on Bentota's beaches, under conditions that are respectful to the animal.

We urge our readers who visit the Bentota region to observe sea turtles not to allow themselves to be deceived by other so-called turtle hatcheries located along the coast. In the majority of cases, these are only profit-making operations that require a fee to see young turtles in plastic enclosures. For an extra fee, tourists can also "liberate" young turtles back to the sea. These practices in no way contribute to the conservation of sea turtles; before visiting them, get as much information as you can on the individuals from authorities, local village groups, hotel proprietors, and others, about what groups are behind these initiatives, their real purpose, and what they accomplish.

PRACTICAL INFORMATION

Egg laying takes place mainly from December to February.

TRANSPORTATION

■ BY PLANE. Colombo is served by numerous regular flights departing from European airports. One possibility is to board an Air Lanka flight from London to Madras and then to Colombo.

■ BY CAR. The coastal route that travels from Colombo toward the southern point of the island makes it possible to easily reach Bentota; train connections are also numerous.

The enclosure managed by the Turtle Protection Project in Bentota is called South Bentota Turtle Hatchery. Information can be obtained in Bentota on how to reach it.

DISTANCES

Colombo—Bentota: 50 miles (80 km)

ACCOMMODATIONS

Bentota has been officially designated as a Coastal Resort Area, that is to say a tourist development area especially designed and directed to meet the requirements of Western vacationers. Possibilities for lodging are therefore not lacking, although the majority of hotels are specifically designed for organized groups.

It is also possible to stay in establishments that are quieter and offer more contact with the inhabitants of the region.

CLIMATE

The dry season, perhaps the most appropriate for visiting the Bentota region, corresponds both to our winter and the most important season for the laying of eggs by sea turtles.

TRAVEL CONDITIONS

Access to beaches is generally completely free. Beaches frequented by sea turtles are, of course, those that have not been overly urbanized. It is a good idea to remain relatively cautious about going out alone at night in certain isolated areas, and it is better to be accompanied by residents of the area such as the members of the Turtle Protection Project, for example, for safety reasons (your own). The Bentota station is almost completely geared toward foreign tourists at the present time, but it is still possible to find more traditional places, as well as several areas of relatively natural vegetation in the vicinity. Bird lovers should not miss the opportunity to visit the Brief Garden, a sumptuous estate created at the end of the 1920s by a Singhalese landscape architect; birds abound on the property with its magnificent gardens. The estate is located in Dharga, approximately 6 miles (10 km) from Bentota toward the interior of the island.

Observation Site

Comoros Islands: Grand Comoro and Mayotte

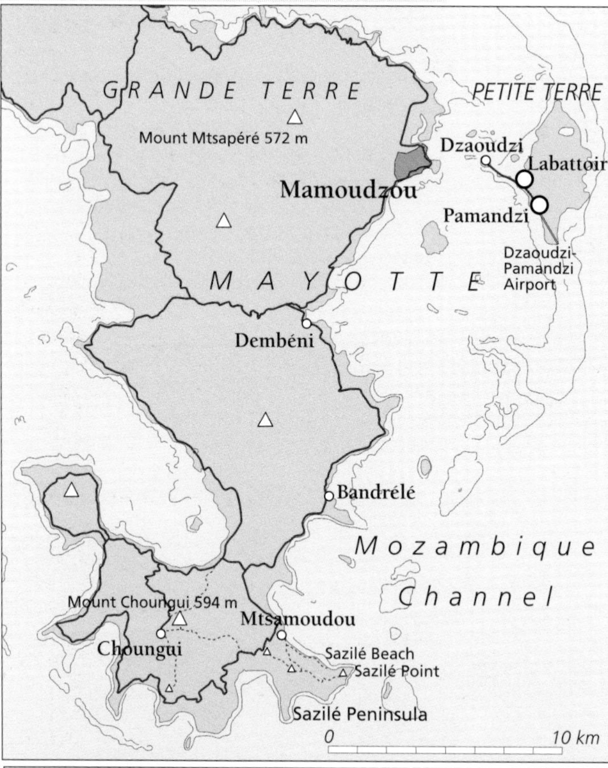

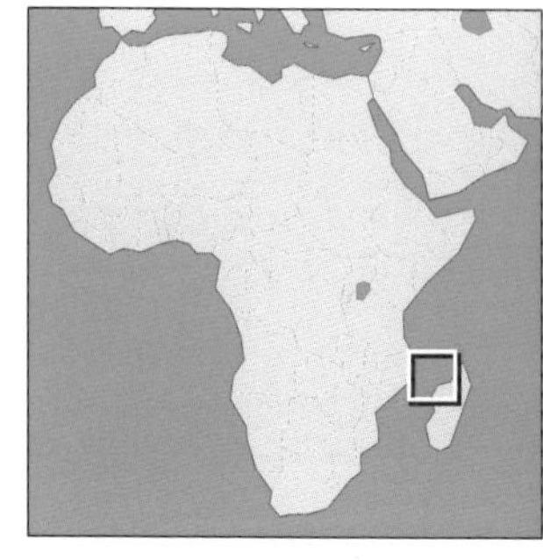

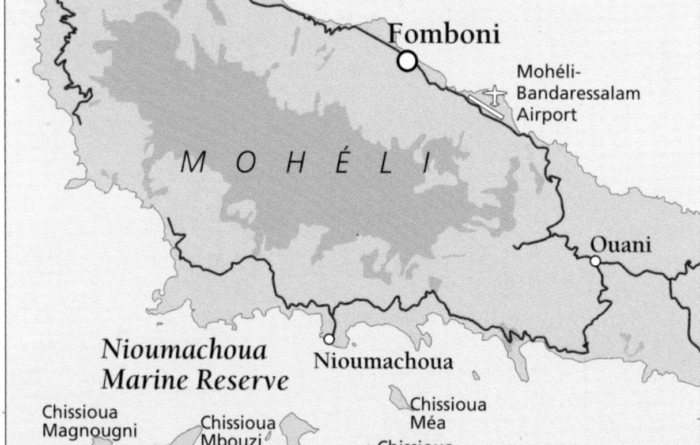

The Comoros Islands are located in the southwest part of the Indian Ocean, in the Mozambique Channel. They extend off the coast of Mozambique, approximately 310 miles (500 km) northwest of Madagascar.

The Comoros Islands are divided into two distinct territorial entities: the Federal and Islamic Republic of the Comoros, which consists of three main islands—Grand Comoro, Anjouan, and Mohéli—and small islands, occupying the major portion of the archipelago, and Mayotte, consisting of the two islands of Grande Terre and Petite Terre, which preferred to remain under French control when the other islands obtained their independence. Today, Mayotte is still part of the French Overseas Territories.

The islands embrace five ethnic groups and two official languages. Since 1975, there have been thirteen coups or attempted coups. Development is hampered by an inadequate transportation system, a young population, and very few natural resources. Like the majority of islands and atolls sprinkled through the Indian Ocean, the Comoros Islands are an important site for the reproduction of various species of sea turtles. Several beaches and bays serve as nesting sites for the turtles throughout the archipelago. The actual possibilities for seeing these animals on land are generally limited as turtle populations have, for centuries, suffered enormously from intense persecution and their total numbers have thus been partially decimated.

The chances for observing sea turtles are, however, rather good on the few sites benefitting from legal protection measures in the archipelago, and these are the sites that we have chosen to present to you.

The conservation of nature barely attracted the attention of the authorities and the Comoros Islands until recently. The destruction of the environment following significant growth and development, as well as tourism and pollution, especially in Mayotte, have moreover involved a certain awareness, relying specifically on programs of sensitization and information for the people in the area.

The Comoros Islands have only a few parks and natural reserves, the latter

The Comoros Islands (here the islet of M'Tsamboro, at Mayotte) is an important place for the reproduction of many species of sea turtles.

View of the Karthala volcano, the highest point on Grand Comoro Island.

primarily geared toward the protection of coastal marine environments, and specifically of sea turtles. While tourist infrastructures are quite limited at present, these sites still offer the best possibilities for the discovery of fauna and of sea flora.

Fauna and Flora

Land fauna and flora are relatively poor in species in the Comoros Islands, as on all oceanic islands. Deforestation has, unfortunately, considerably reduced the area of natural forest; it is believed that at present, only about 15 to 20 percent of the area of the archipelago is still covered with forest, the rest having been occupied by more or less intensive agriculture such as rice, vanilla, ylang-ylang (a type of fruit tree), and so on. Those forests that remain, however, contain a high number of endemic species or subspecies, particularly of avifauna. One of the most interesting animals of the Comoros Islands is the maki *(Lemur fulvus mayottensis)*, one of the rare species of lemur living outside of Madagascar. This lovely animal can often be seen, specifically near certain hotels, where it has become rather familiar.

The Comoros Islands have some very good sites for diving, although facilities remain rather limited, except perhaps in Mayotte. Good possibilities for hiking also exist in the Comoros Islands, specifically on Grand Comoro, where one can climb the Karthala volcano, the highest point on the island at 7,741 feet (2,361 m), in Mohéli and Anjouan, where there are various opportunities for hiking in the forest and mountains to craters, lakes, waterfalls, and so on, as well as in Mayotte, to Mount Mtaspéré, Mount Choungui, or along the Sazilé peninsula.

The Frances sparrowhawk, *Accipiter francesi brutus,* is a typical bird from the islands in the Indian Ocean.

Perhaps the best known "resident" of the Comoros is the ancient fish, the coelacanth. Known only from fossil remains, the discovery of a living specimen in 1938 caused a worldwide sensation among scientists. Cetaceans are also rather numerous in the waters off the archipelago; several species of dolphins can currently be seen, specifically along the northeast coast. Great whales also pass by, sometimes very close

A Strange Legend

Sea turtles are doubly protected on Mayotte and neighboring islands. First, because the Mahorais are Muslim, and this religion prohibits the consumption of the meat of reptiles, then because an ancient and curious custom claims that if one touches a turtle, the shells will push you in the back! The Mahorais are afraid of contact with any turtle, whether land or sea. This fear guarantees the protection of animals but sometimes complicates the work of researchers. In fact, it is difficult for naturalists to recruit a Mahorais, as they are always afraid of contact with these shelled animals. Massacres of sea turtles are occasionally noted, but these may be killings by non-Muslims, or by the inhabitants of Anjouan, the neighboring island, where the superstition is less strong.

The mayotte maki *(Lemur fulvus mayottensis)* is the only species of lemur living outside of Madagascar.

to the coast, near Grand Comoro and Mohéli. The majority of observations are made during the months of May when there is migration to the north, and October, with migration to the south.

Observation

The two sea turtle species that are most frequently found in the Comoros Islands are the green sea turtle and the hawskbill. They lay their eggs at several sites, but never in large numbers, and egg laying takes place more or less throughout the year. The peak season for the observation of these turtles is during our winter. In Mayotte, a plan for the creation of a national marine park on the Sazilé peninsula has been planned for a number of years in order to protect sea turtles that use the beaches of this peninsula located south of Grande Terre. A small observatory has already been established that serves as a base for several researchers who follow the laying of eggs by sea turtles. The marine reserve of Nioumachoua (Mohéli), the first created in the Comoros Islands, was for a long time the only protected site on the archipelago. It was specifically designed for the protection of sea turtles, primarily the green sea turtle, but also the hawksbill. An awareness campaign is underway that has modified, to a certain extent, the perception the inhabitants have of these animals. The best site for the observation of the nesting of sea turtles is the isle of Chissioua Ouénéfou, located a short distance from the coast. The coastal and marine environments of the reserve are among the richest in all of the Comoros Islands, and the landscapes are breathtaking. It is possible to camp on the island's beach, and to easily observe the nocturnal activities of the turtles, while behaving in such a way so as to not disturb them. This includes no flashlights on the beach (you can see amazingly well once your eyes have adjusted to night lighting), no flash photography, and no disturbance of the turtle as she comes ashore to lay her eggs. A visitor's permit is required to be able to enter the marine reserve and to stay there. The Comoros Islands are also one of the best areas in the world for the observation of turtles underwater; the great bays of the island of Mayotte, in particular, often make it possible for divers to admire sea turtles a short distance from the coast, in the enchanting and colorful environment of the great coral reefs.

PRACTICAL INFORMATION

TRANSPORTATION

■ **BY PLANE.** Flights to the Comoros Islands are clearly less frequent and less easy than for other islands in the Indian Ocean such as the Seychelles, Maurice, or Réunion. Air France is the only European company to make regular flights throughout the year to the Comoros Islands (Moroni airport, Grand Comoro), via Nairobi, Madagascar, or the Seychelles. For Mayotte, a stopover in Morona, or in Réunion, with daily flights provided by Air Austral, is inevitable. The Mayotte airport is located on Petite Terre (Pamandzi). You may also wish to check with two other airlines flying to the Comoros Islands: Air Australia and Air Madagascar.

■ **BY FERRY.** Ferry service regularly connects the various islands of the Comoros archipelago; there are also connections between Anjouan and Mayotte.

■ **BY TAXI.** The Sazilé peninsula is located at the southern point of the island of Mayotte, some 18 miles (30 km) from Mamoudzou, arrival point for ferryboats; the Nioumachoua marine reserve is located at the extreme east of the island of Mohéli, approximately 15 miles (25 km) from Fomboni, the island's administrative center. The most practical option for reaching the two suggested sites is to have your own vehicle, but this is rather expensive in the Comoros Islands, especially in Mayotte. You can rent a taxi upon arrival on the island (Mamoudzou in Mayotte, and Fomboni in Mohéli), and it is advisable to arrange with the driver for the return trip. This option, although expensive, is still cheaper than renting a car.

■ **BY BUSH TAXI.** This is the most democratic option, and the one that makes it possible to better discover certain aspects of local life; these group taxis leave regularly for the various parts of the islands, departing from the principal centers. The rates are inexpensive, but the trip is generally much longer, with numerous detours and uncomfortable conditions. The waiting time for the return can sometimes also be very long. To reach Sazilé peninsula, one stops off in the village of Mtsamoudou, a few miles away; after that, the possibilities for public transportation are uncertain. The Nioumachoua marine reserve is reached from the village of the same name. It is possible to get information in the village about the possibilities for reaching the islands in the reserve, and to arrange to rent the services of a dugout or small boat.

■ **BY GUIDED TOUR.** Some travel agencies, located in principal cities, offer guided tours for visiting the suggested sites; since the demand is relatively low, it is better to go several days in advance in order to be able to perhaps benefit from the presence of other visitors and thus to share expenses.

ACCOMMODATIONS

The Comoros Islands, principally Mayotte, are very expensive; establishments rated average or below are rare there, and camping is often discouraged, with no facilities available. There are a sufficient number of hotels in the large centers.

On the other hand, it is possible to spend the night inexpensively in the villages of Mtsamoudou and Nioumachoua, departure points for trips to the sea turtle nesting sites. You can either stay with a resident or plant your own tent close to these villages. You will have to be extremely self-sufficient; in other words, bring with you everything you need for camping, drinking, and eating.

CLIMATE

Temperatures vary little throughout the year in the Comoros Islands; they are generally around 77° to 86°F (25° to 30°C) in midday with little difference at night. The dry season, which extends from April–May and October–November is the peak time for visits; during the humid season, in fact, the temperature is higher, and the air extremely heavy.

TRAVEL CONDITIONS

Access to the beaches of the Sazilé peninsula is free for the moment, perhaps changing when the marine park becomes official. Information may be obtained from the Department of Agriculture and Forestry or from the Tourist Office in Mamoudzou.

A permit is required for the Nioumachoua marine reserve: this can be obtained in Fomboni, the main village on the island of Mohéli, by writing to the Ministry of Rural Development and the Environment, or the Immigration Department.

The Olive Ridley Sea Turtle

(*Lepidochelys olivacea*)
FRENCH: Tortue olivatre, tortue de Ridley

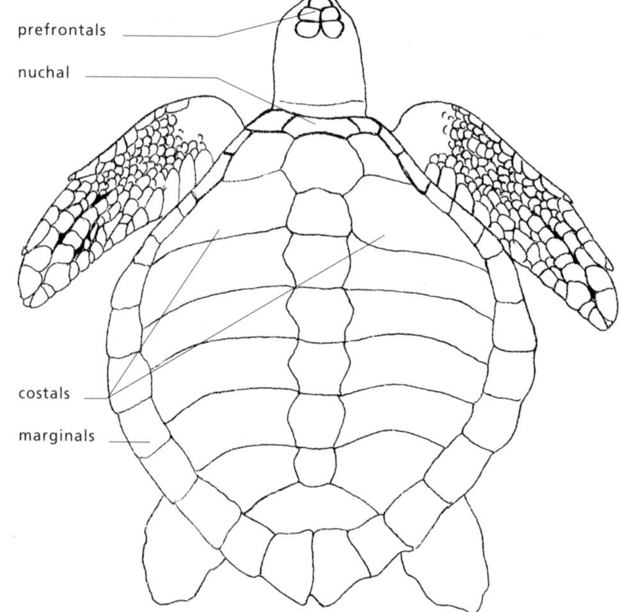

Drawing of the differentiation of the *Lepidochelys olivacea:*
- Nuchal in contact with the first costals.
- Four or five prefrontals.
- Width almost equal to length.
- On the front flippers, there are five to six rows of small scutes between the large plates.
- Pores on the four pairs of inframarginals, between the bridge and the plastron.

Description

Measurements: 29.5 inches (75 cm) maximum.
Average weight: 99 pounds (45 kg).

This turtle is smaller, cordiform, and almost as wide as it is long.

The **back** is rather triangular, with a strong separation above the fore flippers, and a rather flat, elevated nuchal area giving a characteristic "peaked" look. Subadults have one vertebral keel, old individuals a very smooth carapace, with rounded marginals, which gives them the appearance of a stone worn down by time. The general color is from green to ocher-beige with yellow edges in the early years, then, with age, dirty brown, metallic gray, or almost black, barely discernable plates, although outlined with a very fine, lighter-colored edge. The first costals continue to touch the nuchal area, but receding and separating the neck, giving the head more mobility. There are between five and nine vertebrae, sometimes more. The costals can also exceed the normal number, sometimes in different number according to the sides but never more than a difference of two, in certain populations such as the east Pacific, perhaps due to genetics. There are between 12 and 14 marginals. This species is not identifiable by its shell, but by its color and generally peaked shape, its indented back, and its detached neck.

It has a whitish **plastron** in the early years, then greenish or yellowish, or even light gray, having two longitudinal crests particularly prominent in juveniles. There are four inframarginals at the bridges. The top of the flippers and neck are gray-green to dirty brown; the underside is the same color as the plastron.

The **head** is of average size, triangular, with a short muzzle and strong mandibles. It has small eyes, rather unremarkable facial features, and small **flippers**, with two claws. Males, in addition to a wide, long tail, have a curved claw on each front flipper.

Distribution

This turtle is seen worldwide, but the distribution is not as wide as that of other sea turtles; it is found in tropical waters close to the coast, around East Africa and Asia and as far north as Australia, and around South America, above the Tropic of Cancer. It is also found off the west coast of North America, but not on the east coast, the North Atlantic, or in Mediterranean waters, and not south of Australia.

Diet

Some would classify this turtle as an opportunistic carnivore and others as definitely a carnivore. Its jaws evoke a robust eater; it feeds on jellyfish, mollusks, crustaceans, sea urchins, and fish, often in the shallow waters off the coast where it can be observed; in the water, however, it is quick and less visible than the green sea turtle. At sea, it can occasionally be found in groups, warming themselves on the water's surface.

Mating

Sexual maturity occurs early—at seven to nine years for females. Fewer couplings take place opposite the egg-laying beaches, unlike other species, and that often takes place on the high seas. Mating lasts from one to three hours, and males attach themselves particularly well to the backs of the females thanks to their curved claws, hence the characteristic worn spot on the marginals of certain females.

Egg Laying

The olive Ridley sea turtle is a light and very lively species that leaves the water and lays eggs quickly, and returns to the water as soon as possible. All of its movements are lively and efficient, and egg laying can last between 20 and 40 minutes. Most astonishing is the manner of covering up the nest, using swift movements from left to right, of the entire body. In several minutes, the ground is well packed, and the turtle returns once again to its marine environment. If you see it on a beach, you will immediately recognize its speed. Do not move, and do not disturb the turtle. This is a valiant and courageous little turtle that deserves all our admiration.

This species sometimes lays its eggs alone, in the middle of the night, at high tide, on beaches in Micronesia, northern Australia, Indonesia, Malaysia, Sarawak, Bonin Islands, southern Japan, Vietnam, Pakistan, the Seychelles, Sri Lanka, Mozambique, northern Madagascar, Panama, Colombia. In the Atlantic, the egg laying, less numerous, is seen from Senegal to the Congo, and Brazil, French Guiana, Trinity, and Venezuela, but never in the Mediterranean. Approximately every two months, a strange churning agitates the waters opposite certain beaches and 10 turtles climb the beach, then 100, then 1,000, traveling across each other on the sand in a surrealistic ballet, to lay their eggs. During these *arribadas,* turtles arrive in a large group on a single beach, with the egg-laying area completely covered with females. The principal ones take place in Costa Rica (Ostional) and in India (Orissa), but also in Mexico (Jalisco, Guerrero, Oaxaca). During the 1970s, totals of 40,000 to 100,000 turtles per *arribada* were suggested, and 158,161 nests were counted in Ostional in three weeks! Today the *arribadas* are more modest, certainly due to the intensive collection of eggs. It is not known how the animals can come together in the same place for a rather regular egg-laying ritual.

Females lay one to three clutches per season, with intervals ranging from 17 to 29 years. Nests have only one hole, from 19 to 24 inches deep (50 to 60 cm), capable of containing from 30 to 170 eggs. Eggs are smaller than those of other turtles—1.6 inch (40 mm) in diameter—are spherical and white, with a wrinkled membrane. Incubation can last from 46 to 62 days, but the turtles sometimes wait two or three days before leaving together. The newborns have a more elongated carapace than that of adults, with a size of 1.6 to 2 inches (40 to 50 mm). Three keels are visible on the back, and four longitudinal crests under the plastron. Their color ranges from dark gray to dark green, with a white mark on the supralabial shell. The shells and the edges of the flippers are underlined in white. Nothing is known about where the subadults live or anything about their entire lives. It is thought that some mating occurs offshore, after the eggs are laid and the females return to sea. The hatchlings are highly carnivorous.

A leatherback and an olive Ridley have arrived at the same beach to lay their eggs.

Conservation

This species was exploited for its skin and for its meat, but it is the collection of its eggs that endanger its survival; all of the beaches where the *arribadas* took place have seen their populations decline by half or two thirds. At other sites, its survival is compromised by urbanization, the various disturbances caused by man, or the collection of adult animals. In Surinam, Eilanti, where 500 females laid their eggs during the 1950s on less than a mile (1 km) of beach, 25 years later only 40 females were counted. In India, around Orissa, turtles are collected every night to be sent to the capital. In addition, some countries, such as Japan or even Italy, import their most delicate leather—its shells are very small—from Mexico, Ecuador, or Pakistan. The attraction of these eggs is so strong among many coastal ethnic groups that it is difficult to change their customs. To preserve the species, monitoring of nesting beaches is required, limiting the collection of eggs and females.

Observation Site

Costa Rica: Ostional National Refuge

The Ostional site is located along the Pacific coast of this small Central American country. The hawksbill, the loggerhead, and the leatherback sea turtles all lay their eggs there in rather limited numbers. The green sea turtle is not found there, but it is possible to occasionally observe the black sea turtle.

Seen most often is the olive Ridley that frequents Ostional in large numbers; this beach receives the most important *arribadas* on earth, and up to 150,000 olive Ridley sea turtles can arrive there to lay their eggs in only a few days.

The *arribadas* of the olive Ridley turtle, moreover, constitute the principal, if not only, reason for justifying the creation of the Ostional National Refuge. The reserve is seen, in fact, as a narrow strip of land extending parallel to the coast along 5 miles (8 km), between the sea and the areas occupied by humans, occasionally only a few hundred feet wide. The total land area of the sanctuary for olive Ridley sea turtles covers less than 494 acres (200 ha) in total. The Ostional refuge also includes areas of mangroves located at the mouth of the Rio Nosara, a river that empties into the sea at this spot.

Despite its rather modest dimensions, the Ostional site constitutes, along with that of Nancite, which is located in the Santa Rosa National Park, also along the Pacific coast, in the northern part of the country, the principal nesting place for the olive Ridley sea turtles in Costa Rica, and one of the most

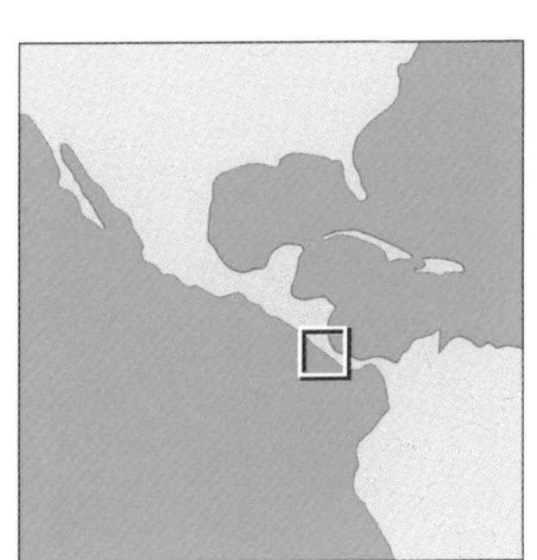

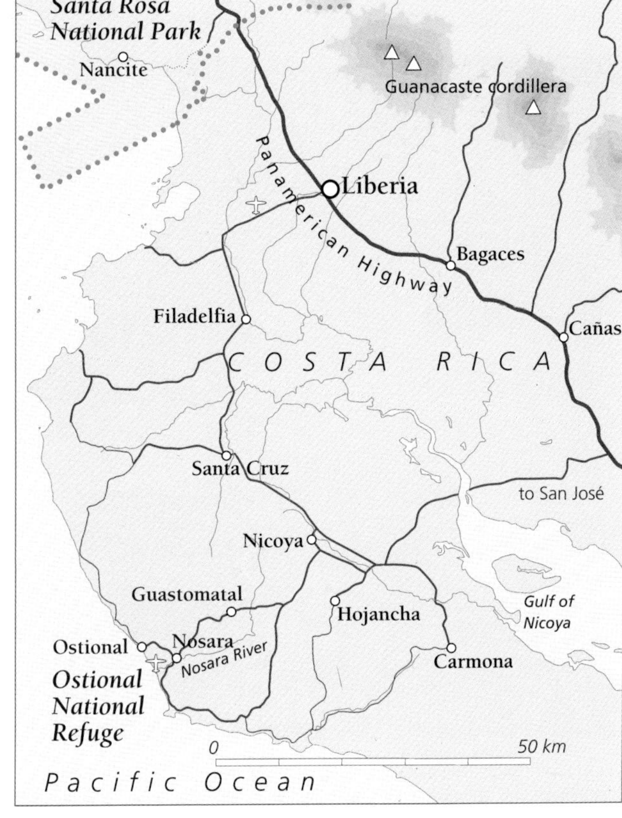

The typical mangrove environment in the Ostional refuge in Costa Rica is home to birds and reptiles.

Urubus waiting patiently for this olive Ridley sea turtle to finish laying her eggs, in the hope of being able to take advantage of eggs that are not well buried.

important sites for the species on the American continent.

Unfortunately, the populations of the species have suffered greatly from the collection of eggs. For a long time, coastal inhabitants have had the habit of pillaging the nests for their personal consumption, which can only have a negative impact on the turtle populations. However, progressively, with the improvement of transportation and of conservation, large-scale commerce was established, and coastal villages supplied cities in the interior with turtle eggs, considered by many in Costa Rica a real delicacy. Fortunately, since 1987, an important and efficient project to protect the eggs has been underway in cooperation with the University of Costa Rica.

Fauna and Flora

The reduced size of the reserve does not allow for an abundant and varied fauna to flourish there. Marine fauna, however, is rather abundant and, in immediate proximity to the beach, especially at low tide, it is possible to observe many marine creatures, of which ghost crabs are the most numerous and the most visible. Crab-eating raccoons are nighttime visitors to the beaches; they feed on crabs, fish, and other small animals.

The areas situated just behind the beaches are covered with wooded or shrub vegetation consisting primarily of deciduous forest, cacti, and so on, often forming a rather dense type of brush. Birds are an attraction in this environment, and one can also hope

PRACTICAL INFORMATION

August through October are the best months to observe the olive Ridleys.

TRANSPORTATION

BY PLANE. The airport at San José, the capital of the country, is linked to several U.S. cities by regular flights.

The Refugio Nacional de Vida Silvestre Ostional is located approximately 19 miles (30 km) from Nicoya. The latter can be reached from national Route No. 1, which links San José to Liberia in the north, in the province of Guanacaste, but this trip requires passage on a ferry. Having your own vehicle considerably facilitates and accelerates the trip from, for example, San José or other large cities. Note, however, that visitors who go to Ostional on their own may experience some difficulties in orientation.

BY ALL-TERRAIN VEHICLE. The final miles from the town of Guastomatal are done on a road that can be *very* difficult to navigate following heavy rains. Also, access to the reserve and to the village of Ostional can prove to be problematic in the rainy season, when the waters cause the overflowing of some small rivers and streams that must be crossed to reach Ostional. An all-terrain vehicle can therefore prove to be indispensable.

BY BUS. It is possible to reach the reserve by bus during the dry season, but the connections from Nicoya can be uncertain, and even impossible, during the rainy season.

BY GUIDED TOUR. Most travel agencies in large Costa Rican cities can organize group excursions to Ostional, especially during peak sea turtle nesting season.

DISTANCES

San José—Guastomatal: approximately 155 miles (250 km) by road.

Ostional—Guastomatal: 6 miles (10 km).

ACCOMMODATIONS

It is possible to camp in the reserve, but there are no amenities for campers. You can purchase certain basic items in the village of Ostional, but it is better to be as self-sufficient as possible if you are planning on camping in the reserve.

There are also pleasant, inexpensive bungalows in the village of Ostional, but at a very basic level of comfort. No other hotel accommodations are available in the area of the reserve.

CLIMATE

Peak nesting season for olive Ridley sea turtles takes place during the rainy season. Rain is frequent and often heavy. Average temperatures are around 77° to 86°F (25° to 30°C) during the day, decreasing very little at night.

TRAVEL CONDITIONS

Access to the beaches of the reserve are lightly regulated: often, it is the villagers who, for a negotiated fee, can guide visitors to the best sites.

to see green iguanas, coatis, and monkeys. Urubus (vultures), fearful predators of young turtles during their emergence, are numerous on the site.

Observation

While it is possible to observe sea turtles on the beaches of the reserve (Playa Ostional and Playa Nosara) at almost any time during the primary nesting season, which runs from June to October for the olive Ridley sea turtle, the *arribadas* remain more irregular.

The best time to see a massive appearance is around September. The *arribadas* last approximately one week, and can be repeated every three to four weeks during the peak nesting season. The precise periods, however, are impossible to predict, as the *arribadas* can be separated by several weeks from one year to the other. The inhabitants of the village of Ostional claim that the olive Ridley sea turtles prefer to wait for the darkest nights, which has not been either proved or disproved by scientific research conducted from year to year on-site by Costa Rican scientists.

The villagers are helpful in guiding visitors to the best sections of beach for the observation of the turtles, and often they know a great deal about the habits of these animals. Most of the guides speak passable English and manage to convey a lot of information aided by gestures and colorful expressions.

A Good System of Self-sufficiency

Since 1987 and the implementation of a conservation program for olive Ridley turtles alone, the inhabitants of the small village of Ostional still have the right to collect eggs on the protected beach, to consume them, and even to market them outside the village. Each villager over the age of 15 is a member of a local cooperative called the Ostional Development Association. This cooperative authorizes the collection of eggs during the first 36 hours following the *arribada,* as the majority of these nests would have been destroyed by other turtles returning several weeks later. Thus, this initial egg removal has very little influence on the success of reproduction and birth. On the other hand, the eggs deposited later are completely protected. The men search for the nests, and the women collect the eggs. Sacks are filled high on the beach, than carried on horseback to a well-guarded warehouse. Children clean the beach to prevent pollution and insects from killing the still viable embryos. The collected eggs are then sold to the government, for a very small amount of money. They are offered for sale in bakeries or directly to Costa Ricans, who eat them raw or spiced with salsa, seasoned with beer, or even in an omelet. Exporting them is prohibited, as this product is protected by international laws. A part of the money received helps the villagers to live; another part is invested in schools, clinics, and roads. In this way, the rapid decline of a species is hopefully prevented while creating a local economy. In 1997 only 676,800 eggs were collected in this manner, or 2 percent of the total number of eggs laid.

The famous *arribadas,* always impressive, bring together thousands of olive Ridley sea turtles, which all lay their eggs on the same beach.

Observation Site

India (State of Orissa): Bhitar Kanika Sanctuary

Approximately 249 miles (400 km) south of the famous region of the Sundarbans at the mouth of the Ganges, this relatively unknown sanctuary is home to another site of *arribadas* by the olive Ridley sea turtle. The state of Orissa itself contains the largest nesting population of the species in the world, with over 200,000 females. The coast of the State of Orissa, the southernmost part of the east coast of India, has retained its frankly rural character; industrialization, which devastated the natural coastal environments of a larger and larger portion of the northeast coast of India, seems in fact to have saved this section of the coast until now. In the interior, green countryside stretches almost endlessly, and here and there, significant forests can still be found as far as the buttresses of Eastern Ghats, the average-sized mountain chain that rises some distance from the coast following a north-south direction. The turtles here suffer from human persecution and modern fishing methods, especially shrimp trawlers; in addition, several major construction projects for industrial fishing or commercial ports threaten the coastal environment that has often remained, until now, amazingly intact in this region. Fortunately, efforts have been underway for a number of years for the conservation of nature. This is how all species of sea turtle came to be protected by Indian law and how various sanctuaries were created, such as that of Bhitar Kanika, which is home to one of the largest beaches in India, Gahirmatha Beach, where each year some 200,000 olive Ridley turtles come to lay their eggs.

The Bhitar Kanika Sanctuary, on the northern coast of Orissa, was created in 1975; it is one of the most important protected sites on the Orissa coast, with 160,550 acres (65,000 ha) of coastal lands, including large masses of mangroves, in the estuary of the Brahmani River.

All of the plants and animals in the sanctuary are, in theory, protected. However, the lack of land development in the vicinity has been up to now the best guarantee for the survival of the olive Ridleys.

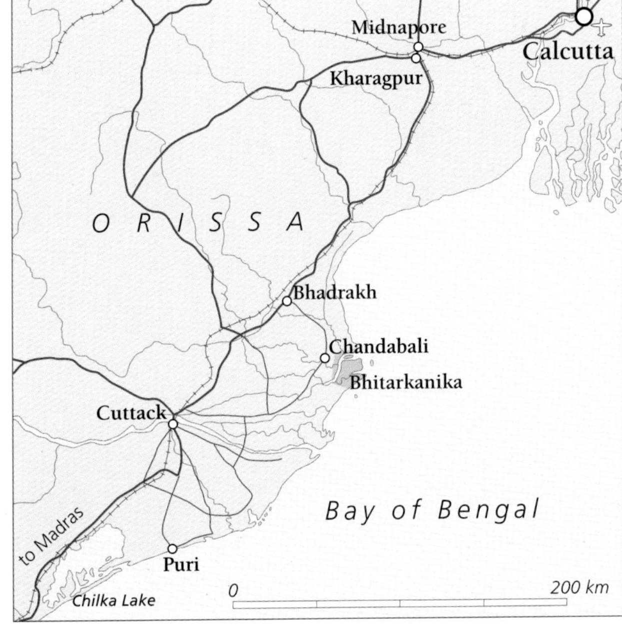

Fauna and Flora

The fauna that populates the sanctuary is typical of species that prefer coastal environments. Four other species of sea turtles frequent the Indian subcontinent and, potentially, all can be seen in the coastal waters of the State of Orissa: the green sea turtle, the hawksbill, the loggerhead, and the leatherback. However, they nest there only rarely, sometimes not at all, as in the case of the leatherback, green sea turtle, and loggerhead.

The avifauna is rich in species, both marine, coastal, and terrestrial. Aside from birds, the other inhabitants of the natural environments of this reserve generally do not allow themselves to be easily observed. The sea crocodile, the largest species of crocodile in the world, is, however, the exception to this rule, since it is not unusual to be able to observe certain individuals. Highly adaptable, this species lives as well in coastal areas as in deltas, estuaries, and even in brackish water rivers; it does not hesitate to attack livestock when it has the chance, and each year causes a certain number of human deaths.

The principal attraction of the Bhitar Kanika remains, however, the olive Ridley turtles.

Approximately 124 miles (200 km) further south along the coast, near the village of Purl, Lake Chilka is another very interesting natural sight on the Orissa coast. This shallow, brackish lake, which is separated from the sea only by a narrow string of short dunes, is one of the most extensive in all of India at 43.5 miles (70 km) long and 9 miles (15 km) wide. The aquatic avifauna there is very rich, particularly during the migratory passages and in the winter; large concentrations of birds spend the winter on the lake from November to February.

The large variety of bird species seen here is partially due to the mixture of brackish and sea habitats, which provides food and shelter for land and oceanic birds.

Tropical waters, warm and calm, are greatly appreciated by sea turtles (shown here, a green sea turtle).

Observations

Egg laying by olive Ridley turtles takes place throughout the year, but in rather limited numbers. The high season, during which the celebrated *arribadas* take place, corresponds to our winter. The months of February and March are the best time for the massive arrival of turtles, but it is impossible to predict the precise moment.

The *arribadas* take place during the night, but often, many olive Ridley sea turtles are still on the beach at daybreak, which then facilitates the possibilities for observation.

Hunting Illegal Dealers

For years, David Whiting, an English photojournalist, has devoted himself to the study and the condemnation of traffic in and killing of turtles, sometimes at peril to his own life; the revelation of the massacres or the illegal gathering has never been well regarded by the local populations. In the State of Orissa, he has spent many nights hidden in his all-terrain vehicle on the shore in order to film and photograph the collectors who work on the beach. He has thus observed the capture of hundreds of olive Ridley sea turtles at the moment when they come to lay their eggs and are loaded into large trucks. The beach, in early morning, is covered with discarded turtles, all suffering under the sun. Local consumption is significant: The turtles are carved while still alive, and shared among the villagers—if they do not die under the glaring Indian sun. Although they are protected by international law and by the Indian Wild Life Protection Act, this does not prevent either the poaching or the sale in the markets of big cities. Varnished carapaces are also offered for sale in airports to tourists. Substitute products must be found to feed the poor villagers of the region, such as the raising of chickens or goats, which would reduce the consumption of sea turtles, and eventually, the total number of olive Ridley sea turtles would return to its turn-of-the-century level.

PRACTICAL INFORMATION

The *arribadas* mostly take place in February and March.

TRANSPORTATION

■ **BY PLANE.** Air India flies to Madras and Calcutta from New York and Chicago, with connections in Bombay.

■ **BY TRAIN.** The city of Bhadrakh is located on the principal railroad line linking Madras to Calcutta. Rail service is frequent, and makes it easy to reach the city.

■ **BY TAXI.** Regular, but not very comfortable, bus service provides connections from Bharakh with Chandabali, but from there, it is not very easy to reach the sanctuary. The least expensive option is to use the local group taxis, but they do not often make the trip to the sanctuary. It is also possible to charter a taxi to make the trip, and to arrange with the driver for the return trip.

■ **BY CAR.** Renting a car remains a rather expensive option in India; rare are the companies that authorize a rental without a chauffeur and the possibilities of easily finding a car in the small villages near the sanctuary remain rather limited.

DISTANCES

Chandabali—Bhadrakh: 18 miles (30 km).

Bhitar Kanika Sanctuary—Chandabali: 22 miles (35 km).

ACCOMMODATIONS

The Bhitar Kanika Sanctuary has several bungalows that visitors can rent at rather reasonable rates, with basic but adequate comfort. You are advised to provide your own food, as the possibilities of finding it in the area of the sanctuary's administrative center are limited.

Also, you should reserve lodging in the sanctuary's bungalows in advance.

CLIMATE

The principal nesting season for olive Ridley sea turtles corresponds to the best season when the monsoons are finished, precipitation is rare, and the temperatures have not yet had time to climb markedly—between 71° and 86°F (22° and 30°C) during the day. When the wind blows with a certain force from the sea, the evenings and nights can be rather cool.

TRAVEL CONDITIONS

You must have an entry pass to visit the sanctuary. There is no tourist infrastructure and no organized tour to the beach.

The Flatback Sea Turtle

(*Natator depressa*)
FRENCH: chéloné à dos plat

Drawing of the differentiation of *Natator depressus:*
- Very close to *Chelonia mydas,* but only present in Australia.
- Flat back.
- Nuchal does not touch the first costals.
- A single pair of prefrontals.
- Rounded muzzle.
- Very small scutes on the forward flippers, between the large plates on the edges.

Description

Measurements: between 37 and 51 inches (95 and 130 cm).
Average weight: 220 to 330 pounds (100 to 150 kg).

This turtle is a close relative of the *Chelonia mydas,* with whom it was formerly often confused. It is characterized by its unkeeled or flat back, which is sometimes slightly depressed toward the fourth vertebra. Its marginals are serrated in the back, especially in juveniles. The adult **carapace** is covered with a rather thick skin, viscous to the touch, greenish to olive, or tending toward brown, which enables it to pass unnoticed on a bed of algae.

Its **back** has four pairs of costals, with the first pair not touching the nuchale area. Lateral marginals curve upwards, which in profile gives the impression of an indentation in the side.

The **plastron** is cream to yellow, as are the underside of the flippers and the tail, wide at the bridge level, receding in the front and the back and without an anal notch.

The **head** is average, with a slightly prominent beak, less strong than *C. mydas*. The eyes are smaller in the latter, and the edges of the jaws are serrated laterally. There is a single pair of prefrontal scutes along the side, and three postocular. Above the eye are many small irregular scutes—wide and well marked in the green sea turtle. The fore flippers are hardly developed, and covered with a range of large scutes. The head, the bottom of the paws, and the neck are gray or tending toward green.

Distribution

This turtle is almost exclusively carnivorous—consuming sea cucumbers, crustaceans, and invertebrates—unlike the green sea turtle. This perhaps explains why its meat is less tasty than that of its close relative, and why it was not generally eaten by man. Found in northern Australian waters, egg-laying sites are located in Queensland, in the northwest, and up to 25 degrees south latitude.

Diet

Contrary to the green sea turtle, the flatback is almost exclusively carnivorous, feeding on sea cucumbers, crustaceans, and invertebrates. This perhaps explains why its meat is less tasty and why man has been far less interested in eating it. The egg-laying beaches of the flatback sea turtle are located in northwest Queensland for the most part, at just 25° latitude south.

Egg Laying

They dig their nests at the end of the day, at high tide, in two shifts—first a hole the size of the body, then the actual nest 12 to 20 inches (30 to 50 cm) deep. There are four clutches laid per season, with around 50 eggs per clutch (78 maximum), less than in the green sea turtle. The average incubation period is 42 days and the hatchlings, which emerge at night, are rather big—2.4 inches (62 mm). This is also a good way to differentiate birth for the two species; the young green sea turtles are half the size. On the beach of Mon Repos, in Queensland, for example, this species lays its eggs in the company of loggerheads. The latter, measuring 50 percent less than the young flatback turtles, are victims of crabs, which cannot seem to pull the young *Natator* turtles back to their burrows. The same is true for the silver gulls. This species strategy of fewer eggs but bigger juveniles seems efficient at first glance. A specific form of thermoregulation has also been observed, and this turtle appears to spend long hours on the surface in order to warm itself in the sun. Often, birds land on the immobile carapace of this sea turtle.

The young do not have the obvious color of the green sea turtle. The plastron is more yellowish or gray, and, of course, the rear marginals are serrated.

The young bear the same "beakless" face as the adults. They are carnivorous from the start, seeking out and devouring shoreline invertebrates. Their larger size affords them some protection against most predators.

Conservation

This species is the least exploited of all sea turtles for several reasons: Its meat has never been of interest to man—only its eggs are collected—and Australia was never frequented by European navigators. Finally, its relative rarity in comparison with the green sea turtle and the loggerhead has limited its collection. The few slaughterhouses open at the turn of the century were for green sea turtles. Today, this species is studied and protected, as are the other sea turtles.

Observation Site

Australia (Queensland): Bundaberg Beach

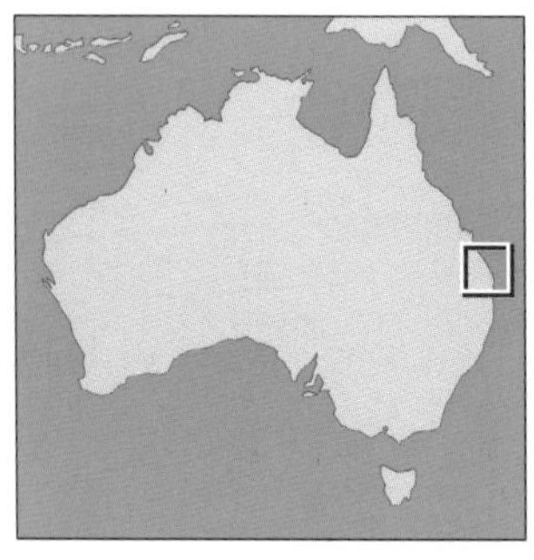

The beach known as Mon Repos, located some 9 miles (15 km) northeast of the coastal village of Bundaberg, an agro-industrial city in the State of Queensland, constitutes one of the principal sites for egg laying by flatback turtles, and one of the best sites for the observation of this species. The region is also at the southern extremity of the Great Barrier Reef, one of the richest coral environments and the most extensive in the world. The abundant sand and coral islands are located several dozen miles north of Bundaberg, and constitute the best sites for sea turtle nesting. Rare are the locations in the region that experience concentrations as large as those on the beach of Mon Repos. Unlike most of the other beaches frequented by sea turtles, it is less sandy and rather rocky, which does not, however, prevent female sea turtles from coming to lay their eggs.

The importance of this nesting site for various species of sea turtles and the interest aroused by these animals in an increasing number of visitors, have caused

the authorities responsible for the protection of nature in the State of Queensland to make it a natural reserve. Not extensive, it is intended above all to protect the nesting beach and to channel the flow of visitors interested in observing the turtles; for instance, there is Fraser Island, a large island located south of Bundaberg, opposite Harvey Bay. This island, almost 43.5 miles (70 km) long but very narrow, looks like a giant bank of sand and dunes. Sea turtles use some of its beaches for nesting, but in reduced numbers, perhaps because of the configuration of the seabed. The northern portion of the island has been declared a national park, called Great Sandy National Park, in order to protect its

The black noddy *(Anous minutus)*, a species of bird in Australia.

After having laid her eggs on the beach at Mon Repos, *Caretta caretta*, handicapped on land like all sea turtles, hurries to return to her preferred environment, the sea.

sand formations and the specific flora and microfauna that thrive there, as well as certain historical remains. It is possible to camp on the island, whose access is subject to an admission fee.

The turtles are most frequently noted in the shallow coastal waters, where their food sources abound and are easier to find.

Fauna and Flora

Sea turtles constitute the principal attraction of the Mon Repos beach, but small living organisms of coastal marine fauna are abundant.

The reputation of the Great Barrier Reef is well known. The main natural riches of this exceptional environment are, of course, found underwater, but the avifauna alone is enough to charm the enthusiast, the Great Barrier Reef being home to some of the largest colonies of seabirds on earth, such as the Australian silver gulls. Sea gulls, terns, gannets, and noddies share the area with frigate birds, Pacific puffins, and white-chested eagles, as well as herons, egrets, avocets, and many other species. The majority of these species of seabirds travel considerable distances and can often be seen in the proximity of Bundaberg.

The waters offshore Bundaberg Beach are known for the annual migration of the humpback whales, from August to October. The village has depicted the whales in a large-scale mural, aptly called the Whaling Wall.

Aborigines and Turtles

Aborigines have occupied Australia for at least 40,000 years. Not very numerous in this vast land, they have never exploited the fauna and have hunted only small numbers of sea turtles, as their people prefer to live inland; in fact, their legends and drawings rarely refer to them. A recent drawing, however, shows a leatherback turtle, easily recognizable by the keels on its back, with a sort of large sac attached to its body. Was this a way for fishermen to avoid having the animal bleed after being killed? In Kakadu Park, near Darwin, several freshwater turtles were painted on the walls. On some, diagonal red streaks evoke the underlying muscles of the animal, which makes one think that the aborigines were familiar with the anatomy of their prey. Today, all turtles are protected on Australian territory and only the aborigines have the right to kill them and eat them solely for their domestic use. This predation is minimal, as aborigines are leaving their reservations and settling near cities. Australia remains the country where turtles are the least exploited and the least collected, whether it is the *Natator depressus*, a sea turtle native to this continent, or *Carettochelys insculpta*, the turtle "with the pig's nose" in the north of the country.

The "sac" attached to this Australian leatherback turtle may be the representation of the *pneuma*, or soul of the animal.

Observation

Loggerhead turtles lay eggs on the Mon Repos beach in greater number, but flatback sea turtles can also be observed there with regularity.

The best time of year to observe egg laying is from December to March, or during the Australian summer. An information center located at the entrance to the reserve and managed by the Queensland Wildlife Department will make it possible for you to learn more about turtles and egg laying, as well as offering suggestions about how to be a respectful visitor.

Access to the beach is free, but guards are permanently on patrol during the peak nesting season, in order to supervise the visitors.

White-tailed eagle *(Haliaeethus leugoscaster).*

PRACTICAL INFORMATION

The most favorable period to observe egg laying is December through March.

TRANSPORTATION

■ **BY PLANE.** There are daily flights from Los Angeles via Qantas, United Airlines, and Air New Zealand to Sydney or Melbourne, with interior transportation then required to reach Brisbane airport.

■ **BY CAR.** The highway that runs from north to south on the Queensland coast passes by Bundaberg, as does the railroad originating in Brisbane.

Car rental in Australia is not expensive and makes life easier for visitors, all the more important as distances are often very long.

■ **BY BUS.** During the peak sea turtle nesting season, private bus or minibus service provides a link between the city of Bundaberg and the reserve. Outside of this period, there is no public transportation available to reach the beach.

DISTANCES

Mon Repos—Bundaberg: 9 miles (15 km).

Bundaberg—Brisbane: 155 miles (250 km).

ACCOMMODATIONS

There are many possibilities for lodging in Bundaberg, from campgrounds to hotels of various categories. Camping is not permitted on the beach or in the immediate vicinity of the perimeter of the Mon Repos reserve.

CLIMATE

The hot and humid season runs from November–December to April–May, needed during the peak season for sea turtle nesting. The rest of the year, the air becomes dryer and somewhat cooler, and rain is rare.

TRAVEL CONDITIONS

The reserve is open to the public all year; it is also open at night during peak nesting season for sea turtles.

There is an admission charge (daily ticket).

The Leatherback Sea Turtle

(*Dermochelys coriacea*)
FRENCH: tortue luth

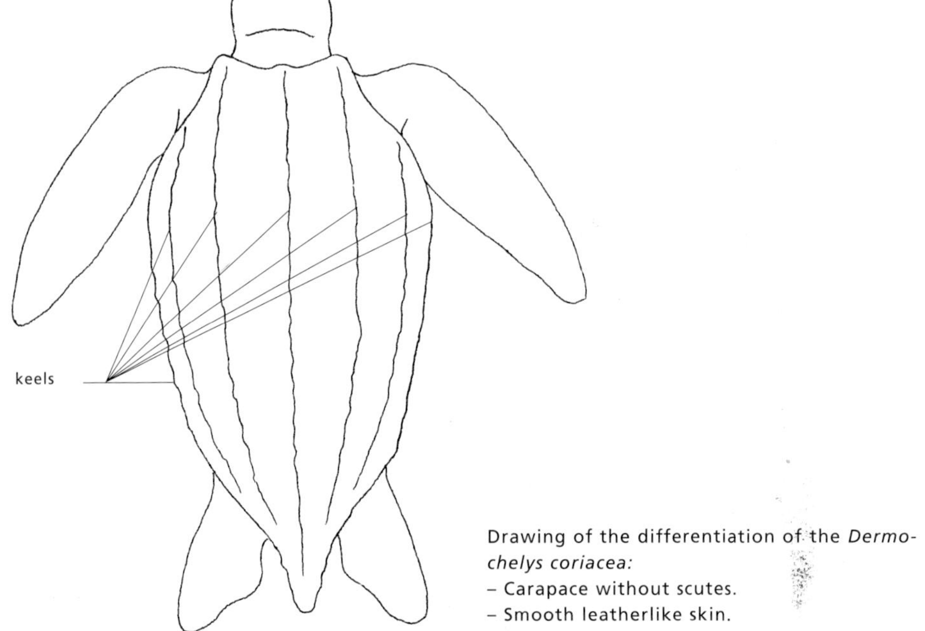

Drawing of the differentiation of the *Dermochelys coriacea:*
- Carapace without scutes.
- Smooth leatherlike skin.
- Five large keels on the back.
- Blue-black color with white spots.
- Pointed behind.
- Massive head with square muzzle.

Description

Measurements: up to 6.5 feet (2 m) in length.
Maximum weight: 2,090 pounds (950 kg).

This is the largest of the sea turtles, differing from the others both in its morphology and its metabolism. It has the unique shape of a lute, with a pronounced triangular caudal point, which gives it additional aquatic aerodynamism. It has a **pseudocarapace** that is covered with a smooth, brilliant skin, midnight blue in color; this "leather," thick and supple, with beautiful texture, has earned it its Latin and English name of "leatherback." On top, there is a thick layer of fat and tissue in which there are bony nodules in the shape of stars that form a mosaic; evolution probably reduced the bony area in this species, to the detriment of a new integument adapted for life in the sea. Its **back** has seven high profile keels, the central one of which is surrounded on the right and left by three keels underlined in a light color and with knobby protuberances. The skin is dark blue to dark gray, with multiple white spots both on the head and on the flippers. These spots must play a role in underwater camouflage, as they evoke spots of light on a dark background.

The leatherback has an enormous **head**, very high and wedge-shaped, with a rather short muzzle. The upper beak is tricuspid, with two strong notches on the sides. Its powerful jaws are used only to chew the jellyfish that are its preferred diet. Its head is

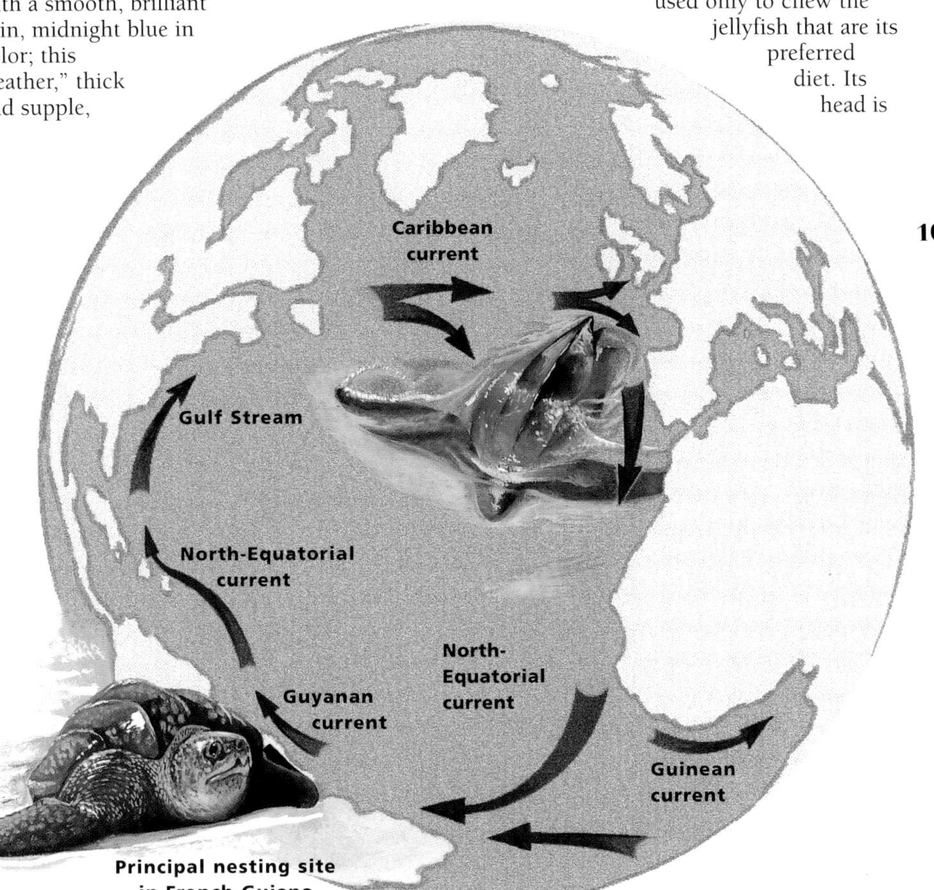

Possible migratory path of the leatherback sea turtle, documented by following marked leatherbacks.

covered with the same leather as the rest of the body; in the parietal area, there is an irregular white mark known as the *chamfer;* it had once been hoped that this could be used to identify each individual before it was understood that the chamfer develops with age. There are conical, soft nodules in the front that are used for chewing prey and also play an important role in oxygenation. During diving, the respiratory cavity is closed up, and the small amount of oxygen needed passes by these nodules into the mouth and the throat. The neck is very wide and short, connecting with the body directly at shoulder level, which makes any flexibility impossible but favors aerodynamism during diving.

This turtle has immense and powerful fore flippers, illustrating the powerful swimming it requires during major migrations, but the muscles at the neck are very robust because, on land, the animal must carry several hundred pounds, which requires a tremendous expenditure of energy. It has a conical tail occasionally with a white keel, which in females does not exceed the length of the carapace, but in males is long and wide at the base. The **plastron** is from white to pink with darker shadows or marks, from under the head up to the tail, with three keels, less visible.

Distribution

This turtle is perhaps the most astonishing of the sea turtles, particularly well adapted to the marine environment. Found in most of the world's oceans, as far as the cold waters of Greenland and Alaska, thanks to its fat and its muscle activity, it can withstand waters of 41°F (5°C). It is a great migrator, and while faithful to certain beaches, it seems to explore the entire world, an individual occasionally traveling from one hemisphere to another. It frequents the Mediterranean, but has not laid its eggs there for many years. It can be seen in France in the channel waters of the Charente, where some are grounded, injured by boat propellers or smothered in fishing nets. Its presence seems to indicate an antediluvian feeding ground, or perhaps even a return to some very ancient nesting grounds.

This is the most pelagic of the sea turtles—it is believed it can descend as far as 1,968 feet (600 m)—and it is never found in low waters or mangroves.

Some have been equipped with tracking devices to follow their migration, but the fact that these turtles dive very deeply, and travel across large distances interrupts the functioning of the apparatus.

The deep-diving characteristics of the leatherback serve to further distinguish it, both in habits and in basic biology, from the shoreline-dwelling sea turtle species.

Diet

It eats primarily jellyfish, which are absorbed in significant quantities. Occasionally, believing it is eating a jellyfish, it eats the plastic bags that are invading the oceans, which causes intestinal obstructions that result in death; therefore, the campaigns against ocean pollution are of immediate interest in protecting sea turtles. It also eats small fish, squid, crustaceans, and mollusks, as well as plants and algae.

Leatherbacks tend to move northward during the summer, following the annual drift of their jellyfish prey.

Mating

Mating takes place in part along the nesting beaches, but it is rare to see it, as the males flee at the slightest approach.

During coupling, the male holds onto the back of the female, thanks to the extraordinary flexibility of its long flippers. At the least disturbance, courtship is interrupted and the animals separate. One fertilization probably serves for all of the clutches that are laid in one season, and perhaps, thanks to the female's spermateca, to eggs laid in subsequent seasons.

Egg Laying

The average number of clutches laid is 4 to 10 per year, but certain females have been known to return to land 17 times; however, it is possible that years with many clutches follow years with only a few. The laying of eggs is spaced from 10 to 20 days apart and can produce 150 eggs. Principal beaches: French Guiana, Costa Rica, Suriname, Guyana, Trinity, Tongaland (Pacific), Florida, Malaysia, and Australia (Queensland). Nesting females have been seen in Africa, from Liberia, Ivory Coast, to Angola. In the Mediterranean, some nesting was formerly noted in Sicily, Libya, Turkey, and Israel.

Today, there does not appear to be any in this area.

Almost all eggs are laid at night at high tide. For these enormous animals, which take two or three hours to lay their eggs and which fear the heat of the sun, working through the night is a matter of survival. Animals that are lost at daybreak or stuck in the mud die rapidly of isolation and exhaustion. Breathing, for this 1,980-pound (900 kg) animal, which must activate the muscles of her flippers first at the same time she moves across the sand is, in fact, exhausting.

Nesting consists of seven phases: ascension (10 minutes; the female stops near the first vegetation); the sweeping the site (15 minutes); the digging of the nest with the hind flippers (25 minutes, resulting in a cavity of 27.5 to 31.5 inches [70 to 80 cm] deep); the actual laying of the eggs (20 minutes; salvoes of many eggs accompanied by harsh and difficult breathing); the filling in of the cavity (10 minutes; the turtle fills the hole and pats down the sand with her hind flippers); the camouflaging of the site by pivoting around; and finally, the return to the sea, which is very variable in length, as the turtle sometimes moves in circles to prevent a predator from finding her nest.

The leatherback sea turtle lays two kinds of eggs: the most numerous, large in size—2 inches (50 mm) in diameter—are white, wrinkled, with a supple membrane, and viable; the others, up to 40 percent of the total, are smaller, softer, more irregular, and seem to have been laid only to "prop up" the principal eggs, as they are nonviable, having no yolk.

The total number of eggs for the season can exceed 1,000, which is a record for chelonians. In the laying phase, the turtle never abandons her work, even if she is disturbed. She is also not very aggressive; a leatherback sea turtle has never been seen injuring anyone, even during the laying of eggs when too many tourists bother her.

The incubation of the eggs varies from 60 to 70 days, and the critical temperature for the eggs is around 85°F (29°C), lower temperatures producing only males

No, these are not juveniles leaving land by the dozens, but large female leatherbacks weighing 1,100 pounds (500 kg), all of which are heading for the beaches of French Guiana at the same time to lay their eggs.

and higher temperatures only females, in a laboratory of controlled enclosure. During egg laying, significant aqueous secretions are noted around the eyes and sometimes the mouth. These are not tears of pain; this emission is required to evacuate the salt absorbed with seawater, to hydrate her eyes, and perhaps to cool off the female's head. Her powerful sighs during egg laying correspond to her difficulty in breathing.

The hatchlings are large-sized juveniles of 2.7 to 3 inches (7 to 8 cm), who already resemble their elders, with seven small keels, white spots on a blue-black background, and gigantic hind flippers, and who hurry to reach the marine environment. Because of their specialization toward a seagoing life, they are perhaps even less adept on land than the other sea turtles. This puts them at a very distinct disadvantage against predators. Many die as a result of attacks by dogs, vultures, or crabs. Eggs can also be eaten by insects, but they are not appreciated by man, perhaps because the flesh of adults is considered nonedible and there have even been cases of poisoning.

When the hatchling reaches the sea, and escapes its aquatic predators, it perhaps returns to the feeding grounds. It is not seen again until it is a subadult, and a leatherback sea turtle less than 31.5 inches (80 cm) is practically never seen in the sea. The growth of juveniles must be rapid, and this size must be reached in only three or four years. The maximum age for this species is not known. It is believed to live about 50 years, which is short in comparison with other turtles. Its migratory, pelagic and varied life certainly implies a limited life expectancy; however, dead leatherback sea turtles have been found, weighing almost one ton, whose carapaces are marked by numerous wounds, which may indicate great age.

Protection

The leatherback is one of the best-studied sea turtles. This is due to its exceptional appearance and its presence in all the oceans of the world. An enclosure existed in French Guiana (Les Hattes) for a long time and tens of thousands of turtles were recorded there and studied. Other sites for study and protection, such as Rantau Abang, in Malaysia, have also contributed a great deal of information on this animal. It was formerly thought that this species was seriously endangered, but now it is believed that the populations of leatherback sea turtles are not experiencing a decline and there is no need to develop enclosures such as the program in French Guiana advised; efforts focus on guaranteeing the maximum amount of tranquility for turtles in their nesting areas.

Problems continue, however, such as pollution from plastic bags and the danger of drift nets. Many old turtles are also found to be marked by terrible wounds caused by boat propellers, harpoons, gaffes, and so on. Finally, even in French Guiana, females are still killed for their eggs, so vigilance continues to be required. In Belize, the Indians living near the beaches are responsible for monitoring them. Those who formerly collected eggs now welcome students or tourists, generating this "economic manna" themselves. It is also hoped that animal protection, too, can become the responsibility of local populations, to provide a better ecological balance between the fauna and the inhabitants of nearby beaches.

Much still remains to be learned about these mastodons of the sea: Where are the feeding grounds for the juveniles? Are they gregarious during their early years, or more individualistic? The idea of real "underwater autoroutes" has been developed, which would make it possible for animals to follow each other at a distance, in the middle of currents and vast expanses of ocean. What happens inside a nest at the moment of birth? How do the young resist ground predators? Adults are also seen leaving the water with a rémora—a type of sucking fish—attached to the "leather," which returns alive to the sea, after having lived for two or three hours in the open air. How is that possible? What is the interdependence among all these animals, small and large?

Observation Site

French Guiana: Yalimapo

The coast of French Guiana up to now has been saved from urbanization and mass tourism, which has already devastated so many of the world's coastal areas. This is due perhaps to its particularly humid climate and especially to the swampy and unstable character of its coast, which evolves and changes constantly under the effect of ocean currents.

Located between the mouth of the Maroni River and that of the Mana River, the beach of Yalimapo (Les Hattes Beach) is currently the most important nesting site of leatherback turtles. The area is rich in sediments carried along by these important rivers, and the shape of the coast changes rapidly, as do the sandbanks located nearby in the sea. Thus, while it is true that leatherback sea turtles did not lay eggs on the banks of the Mana prior to 1950, it is possible that in 30 years the beaches will once again have become too narrow for this species. Currently, however, the conditions on Yalimapo Beach are perfectly suited for sea turtles, and they use it intensely for building their nests. Turtles have long been subject to rather intense poaching in French Guiana, and specifically in Yalimapo. For many years they have been a major dietary item for the local native tribes and a reliable trade object. An important conservation project for these animals was directed for almost 15 years by the French scientist Jacques Fretey and his team; he made possible the reduction of poaching of females and the pillaging of nests.

Yalimapo Beach, as with the swamps of Basse-Mana that extend back from the coast for more than 74,100 acres (30,000 ha), are currently the subject of a plan to classify them as a natural park.

Other isolated beaches in this area of French Guiana, often separated from each

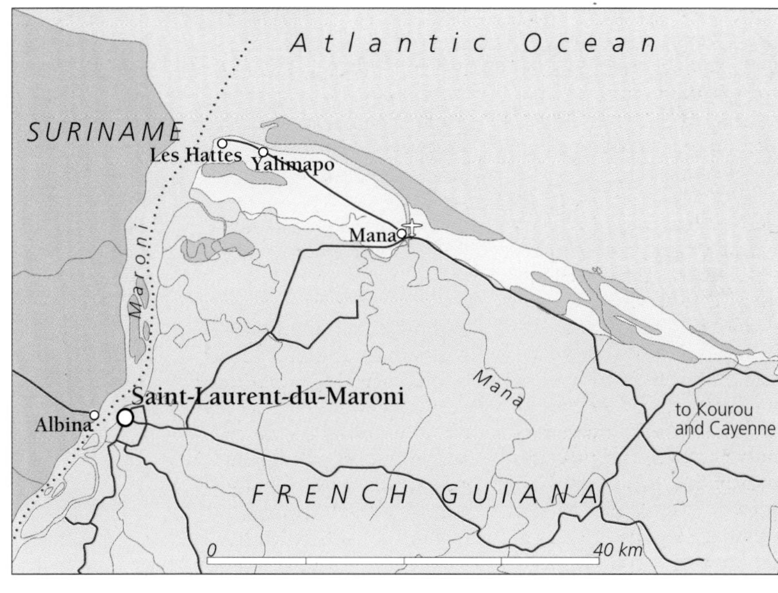

Phylomedusa vaillanti is part of one of the many families of tree frogs in the Amazon forest that almost never leave the trees for the ground. These frogs are common up to 131 feet (40 m) high in the trees.

A narrow strip of sand separates the Atlantic Ocean from the great swamps of Basse-Mana, French Guiana. The outline of the coast, influenced by the ocean currents, is constantly changing.

other by large expanses of mangroves, also play a somewhat important role in the nesting of sea turtles.

Fauna and Flora

While the beach itself is frequented by a relatively small number of animal species, the large swamps intersecting the forests that extend directly behind are home to a rich and varied fauna.

The national park ornithological inventory currently in preparation has already made it possible to identify more than 250 bird species; during periods of migration and wintering, important concentrations of migratory birds—primarily limicoles and small waders—that have come as far as the United States frequent the Basse-Mana region for rather lengthy periods.

The number of mammals here is remarkable; species representative of the coastal forest environments of this part of South America exist side by side with species found far away in the interior of the Amazon forest. The Virginia deer, the tapir, the collared peccary, and the white-lipped peccary are the largest mammals in the area. The crab-eating raccoon is often seen there, as is the opossum, while armadillos, anteaters and tamanduas, coatis and kinkajous, or the Guyana otter, the agouti, the paca, or the capybara, while present in the area, are often not seen by visitors. Primates are represented by the golden-handed tamarin, the howler monkey, the black capuchin, the spider monkey, the saki, and the squirrel monkey. There are also four species of cats: the well-known and prestigious jaguar, the ocelot, the tiger cat, and the jaguarundi.

Manatees have been noted, both in the river's estuary as well as in the creeks, which are very numerous, and which branch out throughout the swamps. Often, schools of dolphins can be seen a short distance from the coast.

Finally, reptiles, frogs, toads, and other amphibians are also particularly numerous. But the most abundant animal, on the beach as well as in the interior swamp, remains, incontestably, the mosquito!

The best time to see these creatures is at night, when their nocturnal prey becomes active. A walk through the forest with a flashlight will reveal many of their

White egret fishing for small piranhas, in the swamps during the dry season.

intended victims, on the edges of established trails.

Observation

It is easy in Yalimapo to observe sea turtles coming to lay their eggs, leatherback turtles being, of course, the most numerous. Their numbers fluctuate from year to year for reasons that are not currently understood, but some years, the number of females laying their eggs is estimated at between 6,000 and 15,000. They lay their eggs throughout the year in Yalimapo, but the peak season runs from May to July.

Green sea turtles are also relatively common in Yalimapo; egg laying by hawksbill sea turtles is noted almost every year, but in very small numbers. The olive Ridley sea turtle, formerly quite common, continues to frequent this beach more or less sporadically. The presence of loggerhead sea turtles has been noted, but is rather exceptional.

A team of Amerindians from the village were recruited to monitor the laying of eggs throughout the year. A new visitor's center has also been constructed on the edge of the beach but it is not yet in operation; it includes an egg incubation unit, a scientific station, lecture rooms, and other amenities.

No means for accompanying visitors is currently in place; therefore, it is essential that each visitor use common sense when on the beach at night, and behave in such a way so as to not disturb the turtles that are leaving the sea to lay their eggs. The use of lights such as flashlights or camera flashes, specifically, is prohibited. Moonlight is reflected from the nearby water, and night vision is not difficult. Artificial lighting—from any source—and excessive noise are to be avoided. After a while, you will recognize and will be able to identify unfamiliar sounds (such as sand crabs) scuttling nearby.

The majority of leatherback sea turtles prefer to leave the sea to reach the beach in the darkness of night, but there are also some who are still on land at sunrise, while others occasionally come to lay their eggs before nightfall, this occurring most frequently on overcast days.

An arboreal frog (*Phylomedusa bicolor*) perches atop an identically colored flower.

The Amerindians and Turtles

Between the mouth of the Mana and that of the Maroni live the Galibis or Kalina Indians. These are Amerindians of Caribbean origin, like the Wayana and the Trio who have settled in French Guiana since the tenth century. Today there are approximately 1,500 Amerindians in Guyana, and they still live by fishing or cultivating small parcels of cleared land. In Yalimapo (Les Hattes), their village, built above the beach, includes some 30 carbets—roofs protecting hammocks and provisions. They live in close proximity to the beaches and are in permanent contact with the leatherback sea turtles, the eggs of which they long consumed raw, boiled, in omelets, or smoked. Today, the turtles are protected and the Kalibis, no longer able to collect eggs or kill females, have adopted a more classic diet; however, leatherback sea turtles are still found massacred, their bodies cut open with machetes to remove the eggs. Killing a female before she has laid her eggs is totally irresponsible, and the perpetrators of these stupid massacres are said to be refugees from Suriname, who have illegally entered French Guiana.

Today, turtles are protected by the center at Les Hattes and the WWF. Volunteers monitor the beaches, assist tourists, and participate in local life. Perhaps the Galibis Indians could be more directly involved in the protection activities.

PRACTICAL INFORMATION

The village and the beach of Yalimapo are located in the extreme northwest of French Guiana, some 9 miles (15 km) from the town of Mana and in the immediate vicinity of the mouth of the Maroni River on the northern border with Suriname.

TRANSPORTATION

BY PLANE. Arrival in French Guiana from Europe is through Cayenne. Guyana Airways flights depart daily from New York.

BY CAR. The ideal way to reach Yalimapo is, of course, by private car, which is rather expensive in French Guiana. From Cayenne, follow the coastal route in the direction of Saint-Laurent-du-Maroni and turn off toward Mana.

BY TAXI. Public transportation—specifically group taxis—operate quite regularly between Cayenne, the capital, and the town of Saint-Laurent-du-Maroni, located inland along the Maroni River. Transportation to the small town of Mana, however, is less frequent. From Mana, upon request, taxis can continue as far as Yalimapo, which is more expensive.

BY GUIDED TOUR. Many travel agencies in Cayenne organize trips to Yalimapo; there are organized tours specifically designed for the observation of sea turtles.

DISTANCES

Cayenne—Saint-Laurent-du-Maroni: 112 miles (180 km)

Mana—Saint-Laurent-du-Maroni: 37 miles (60 km)

Les Hattes—Mana: 9 miles (15 km)

ACCOMMODATIONS

Carbets maintained by the Amerindians of the village are available. This is the sole option for lodging in the immediate vicinity of the beach and the village. Camping in the wild is not encouraged in the Yalimapo area. In spite of all the precautions you can take, this practice can only prove to be harmful to the tranquility of the turtles that have come to lay their eggs.

Lodging at the visitors' center is the sole alternative, but call in advance to find out if there is room available.

CLIMATE

From December to July there is an anticyclone from the Azores that gives rise to a great many rainstorms. The anticyclone from Saint Helena takes over from August to November, resulting in hot and relatively dry weather.

Temperatures show little variation throughout the year —77° to 81°F (25° to 27°C); they lower very little during the night. Relative humidity is very high; during the rainy season, the air is often saturated.

TRAVEL CONDITIONS

Although the Yalimapo beach is protected by a local government decree, no particular restrictions seem to apply with regard to the frequenting of the site by visitors. Access to the beach is free.

Observation Site

Malaysia: Rantau Abang

The beaches near the fishing village of Rantau Abang constitute one of the most important sites for egg laying by this turtle in Malaysia, and is also the best known and most accessible. Rantau Abang is located in the State of Trengganu, in peninsular Malaysia, on the east coast. In addition to the leatherback sea turtle, Malaysian waters welcome the green sea turtle, the hawksbill, and the olive Ridley sea turtle.

The laying of eggs by leatherbacks in this area has been known for a long time, and for decades has attracted ever-increasing numbers of visitors. Well-controlled tourism can have a minor or negligible effect on turtle nesting areas, to the distinct benefit to the turtles, local settlements, and the tourism industry. The lack of organization and education of visitors that has long characterized the nesting beaches of Rantau Abang represents, unfortunately, an example of the harmful effects that anarchic tourism can have on sea turtles at their nesting sites.

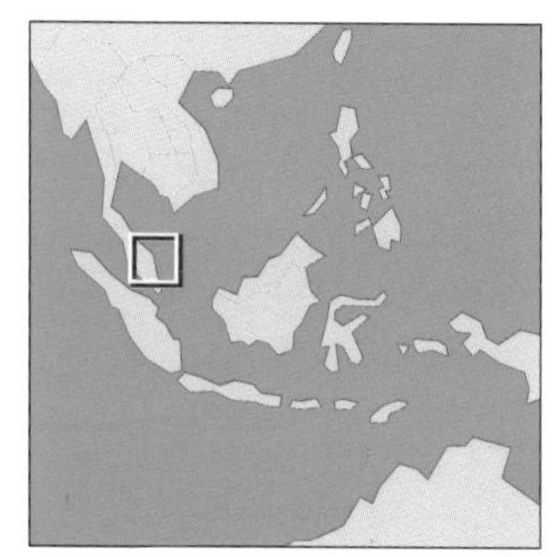

At least 20 years ago, females came by the thousands each year to lay their eggs; today, no more than a few hundred still frequent the site. Scientists have not been able to determine the precise causes of this significant decline; while it is most likely the result of a series of combined factors such as excessive pillaging of nests, killing of the turtles themselves, and losses due to certain fishing methods, it is evident that the influx of

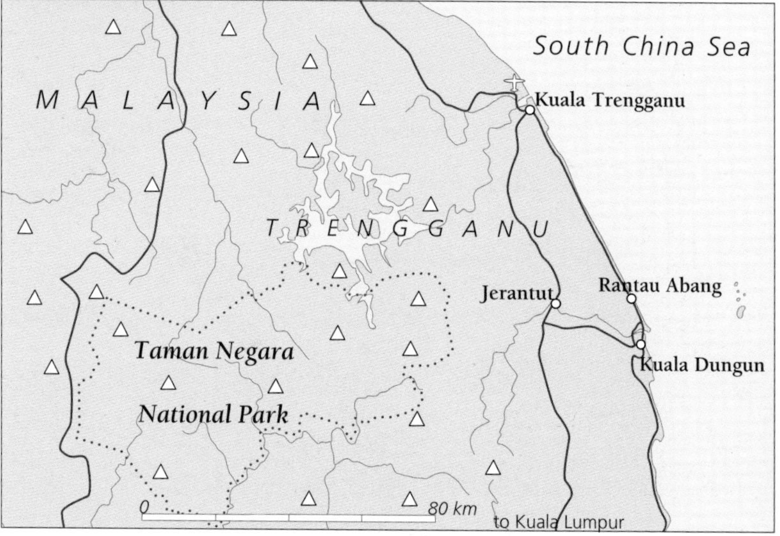

undisciplined visitors has also played an important role.

Several years ago, it was still possible to see groups of several dozen observers surrounding a single leatherback sea turtle. In the light, disturbed, even molested by certain tourists who did not hesitate to sit on its back, even to carve graffitti into its tough skin, it had no other choice than to return to the sea as quickly as its imposing mass would allow.

For a long time, the authorities seemed unaware of the situation, but recently, things have changed, and this time for the better. Tourism centered on turtles continues to attract a significant number of visitors to the village and the neighboring beaches, but a system for educating and monitoring visitors has been implemented by the Department of Fisheries.

In spite of the small number of females that currently come aground to lay their eggs, the beaches of Rantau Abang are still an excellent site for the observation of these strange sea turtles.

Fauna and Flora

As the beaches are located in the immediate vicinity of the village of Rantau Abang, whose surroundings are rather intensely exploited by man, the fauna here is neither abundant nor particularly remarkable. The laying of eggs by sea turtles, in fact, constitutes the sole real naturalist attraction of the site.

On the other hand, approximately 62 miles (100 km) inland there is the Taman Negara National Park. Covering more than one million acres, it is home to the oldest primary rain forest on earth. The forest reaches as far as the eye can see, from 984 to 6,560 feet (300 to more than 2,000 m) of altitude. Various types of forest can be seen, sometimes deciduous, sometimes evergreen, in which meranti and other commercially valuable trees dominate. Higher up, the abundance of ephiphytes and lianas form a profusion of vegetation made possible by very high humidity. Taman Negara is home to some remarkable fauna: the elephant, the

View of the sub-forest of Taman Negara, Malaysia.

very rare Sumatran rhinoceros, the Malaysian tapir, the gaur (a bovine), the wild pig, the sambar deer, the barking deer, the gibbon and various species of macaques, the tiger, the leopard, the panther, and the Malaysian bear. More than 250 bird species, resident or migratory, populate the forest, which is equally high in reptiles and amphibians. To date, no high-canopy studies have been conducted to further explore the richness of the upper rainforest environment. Most travel takes place along the rivers, in motorboats. Many hiking trails also exist, and a certain number of observation towers have been erected in order to improve the chances of observing fauna in the dense forest.

Observation

The leatherback sea turtle is not the only turtle to lay eggs on the beaches of Rantau Abang, where there is also a good chance of seeing green, hawksbill, or olive Ridley sea turtles in season.

The peak season for egg laying by leatherback sea turtles runs from April to

A Diet for Young Leatherbacks

The immense leatherback sea turtle is the only turtle that obstinately refuses to be raised in an aquarium, even in large installations. Two biologists at the Rantau Abang station, Dr. Chang Eng Feng and Dr. Liew Hock Chark, have, however, found a food that the hatchlings accept, which raises the hope that juveniles can be raised. They had already tried, in vain, to feed them morsels of fish or pieces of squid, but finally, it was small wafers, based on squid and gelatin agar, that tempted them. If these wafers, 0.12 inches (3 mm) thick, are allowed to float, a young turtle cannot catch them due to the position of its mouth, but if the wafer is held lightly under the water, the turtle can swallow it whole. Thus, it is hoped that nurseries can be created in a natural environment, with nets, which would make it possible to release animals of a certain size less susceptible to predators.

The Sumatran rhinoceros is a species that is rare and difficult to observe. It survives in the deepest forests of Indonesia.

September. The Rantau Abang region is the only one on the Malaysian peninsula frequented by leatherbacks, a phenomenon that appears to be explained by the configuration of seabeds in the immediate vicinity of the beaches in this location.

Today, some 12 miles (20 km) of beach have been designated as a natural reserve for sea turtles. A visitors' information center has also been opened near the village, with an exhibit and an educational film devoted to sea turtles, where the required information for nocturnal visits to the beach can be obtained.

The reserve is divided into three sections: One is completely closed to visitors—it is here that the guards from the reserve rebury eggs laid by turtles in other endangered areas, the second is accessible to a limited number of visitors, while access to the third is unlimited but the number of turtles that come to lay their eggs there is clearly smaller.

Guards patrol both day and night, in order to prevent any pillaging of nests and to assure that visitors remain at least 15 feet (5 m) away from the turtles, do not use lights, do not build fires on the beach, and so on. A certain number of islands located a short distance from the coast of the State of Trengganu are also frequented by green sea turtles; at present, most are classified as natural reserves.

The watery secretions around the eyes are not tears of pain. Such emanations are necessary to wash away the salt absorbed with the seawater, to hydrate the eyes, and perhaps to cool off the head.

PRACTICAL INFORMATION

April through September are the best observation months.

TRANSPORTATION

■ BY PLANE. The airport of entry is Kuala Lumpur, the capital of Malaysia.

■ BY CAR. From the capital, the park can be reached by road either in a rental car or taxi, public transportation being less practical, via the town of Jerantut. The trip can also be made in a taxi or a vehicle rented in Kuala Trengganu, capital of the state. Visitors must count on between two and three hours of travel. The roads can be difficult to navigate following rain. From this town, there is regular bus service to the park.

DISTANCES

Rantau Abang—Kuala Lumpur: 186 miles (300 km)

Rantau Abang—Jerantut: 15.5 miles (25 km)

Rantau Abang—Kuala Dungun: 12 miles (20 km)

Kuala Trengganu—Kuala Dungun: approximately 50 miles (80 km) by road

ACCOMMODATIONS

A number of rather large local bungalows with relatively basic comfort make it possible to lodge in the immediate vicinity of the village of Rantau Abang and the beach. It is also possible to camp in the vicinity; contact the Information Center at the reserve.

CLIMATE

During the peak egg laying season for leatherback sea turtles, precipitation is relatively low in the area. Average daily temperatures are around 86°F (30°C), with little change at night.

TRAVEL CONDITIONS

An entry pass to the reserve must be acquired in order to reach certain portions of the beach. The Sea Turtle Information Center is normally open from May to September.